hf

The Teaching Assistant's Guide to Numeracy

Also available from Continuum

The Teaching Assistant's Guide to Numeracy

Sara Fielder

continuum

Continuum International Publishing Group

The Tower Building	80 Maiden Lane
11 York Road	Suite 704
London, SE1 7NX	New York, NY 10038

www.continuumbooks.com

© Sara Fielder 2007

British Library Cataloguing-in-Publication Data
A catalogue record for this book is available from the British Library.

ISBN 0-8264-9606-7 (paperback)

Library of Congress Cataloging-in-Publication data
Fielder, Sara.
    The teaching assistant's guide to numeracy / Sara Fielder.
        p. cm.
    ISBN-13: 978-0-8264-9606-5 (pbk.)
    ISBN-10: 0-8264-9606-7 (pbk.)
    1. Numeration--Study and teaching. 2. Mathematics--Study and teaching. 3. Teachers' assistants. I. Title.
    QA141.F54 2007
    513--dc22

                                2007020999

Typeset by Kenneth Burnley, Wirral, Cheshire
Printed and bound in Great Britain by Athenaeum Press Ltd., Gateshead

Contents

The Teaching Assistant's Guide to Numeracy

Sara Fielder

continuum

Continuum International Publishing Group
The Tower Building   80 Maiden Lane
11 York Road   Suite 704
London, SE1 7NX   New York, NY 10038

www.continuumbooks.com

British Library Cataloguing-in-Publication Data
A catalogue record for this book is available from the British Library.

ISBN 0-8264-9606-7 (paperback)

Library of Congress Cataloging-in-Publication data
Fielder, Sara.
    The teaching assistant's guide to numeracy / Sara Fielder.
        p. cm.
    ISBN-13: 978-0-8264-9606-5 (pbk.)
    ISBN-10: 0-8264-9606-7 (pbk.)
    1. Numeration--Study and teaching. 2. Mathematics--Study and
teaching. 3. Teachers' assistants. I. Title.
    QA141.F54 2007
    513--dc22

                                                    2007020999

Typeset by Kenneth Burnley, Wirral, Cheshire
Printed and bound in Great Britain by Athenaeum Press Ltd., Gateshead

Contents

This book refers to Teaching Assistants; however, we recognize that there are many different names for this important role. So this book is also for Classroom Aides, Classroom Assistants, Educational Assistants, Learning Support Assistants, Paraeducators, Special Needs Assistants, TAs, Teacher Aides and Teacher Assistants.

1

What is numeracy?

Have you ever heard anyone say 'I can't do maths' or 'I am not very good at maths'? You may have even said it yourself. Although things are changing, it still seems more socially acceptable to admit a weakness in subject knowledge or mathematics than it does to say that you cannot read or write, and yet mathematics skills are essential for everyday life. Encouraging children to view mathematics in a positive light might be as much a battle against attitudes established over many years as it is teaching them successfully to understand and apply mathematical learning. As TA an important aspect of your role will be to encourage children to view mathematics positively and develop a 'have a go' attitude.

What does it mean to be numerate?

Reflect on a child who is good at mathematics. What qualities does he or she possess?

It is often assumed that children who quickly and correctly carry out a series of calculations, with very little perceptible effort, are good mathematicians; but this is only part of it. The key to being numerate is applying an understanding of mathematics to real life, in written or verbal problems.

For example, children may be able to quickly carry out:

$$\begin{array}{r} 45 + \\ 73 \\ \hline 118 \end{array}$$

But when asked to work out a bill for £45 and £73 they may fail to recognize the need to add or cannot set out the calculation correctly, muddling up the digits.

Numerate children have an understanding of the position of the number in the number system (this means the order of numbers, i.e. 1, 2, 3, 4 . . . or 98, 99, 100, 101, 102), its relative size (i.e. that 45 is bigger than 44) and the place value of the digits (that 111 is one hundred and ten and one). They will have a general 'feel' for the number.

This confidence then enables them to understand and apply strategies needed for calculations, using an understanding of place value (tens and units). For example:

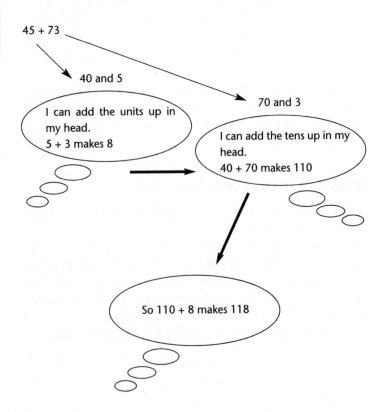

45 + 73

40 and 5

70 and 3

I can add the units up in my head.
5 + 3 makes 8

I can add the tens up in my head.
40 + 70 makes 110

So 110 + 8 makes 118

An experienced mathematician will have a set or series of known facts that can be easily recalled so, for example, they know which two numbers when added will make ten. They also have the confidence to be able to apply these known facts to figure out new facts and work out calculations.

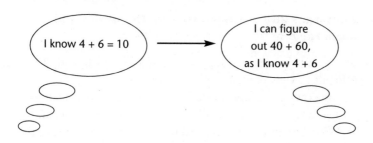

Able mathematicians enjoy the subject; they are excited by the challenge and persevere in the face of problems and questions. They often value their own as well as others' efforts. In your role as TA you may work on extending the gifted and talented or more able mathematician (check on the phrase your school uses to describe the most able). Without your help and the right motivation they may become bored, frustrated and demotivated (see Chapter 8 for information and ideas on supporting more able children).

If this is what it means to be numerate, we now have to consider those children who do not demonstrate levels of numeracy. Around 20 per cent of children leave primary school each year without reaching the minimum expected level of attainment for 11 year olds – and this is where you come in. The majority of your work will be supporting this group of children.

How did you feel about mathematics when you were at school? Thinking about this may help you to understand the attitudes of the children you support.

Numeracy and mathematics, mathematics and numeracy

Mathematics and numeracy are so interlinked that it is very difficult to view them as separate concepts.

Numeracy can simply be defined as an ability to use numbers – to count, order, solve problems, read data, calculate, and so on. Numbers may be used without a context – for example, 5 + 7 – or within the context of time, money or measures – for example, what is the length of the carpet required if part of the corridor was 5m long and the other part of the corridor was 7m long?

Mathematics is the subject as a whole – it includes shape (there is a lot of numeracy involved) and space and all aspects of numeracy.

If you are working in a primary school you may hear that you are supporting numeracy in the mathematics lesson, or mathematics in the numeracy lesson!

At the end of Year 2 and Year 6 children take National Curriculum tests in mathematics. They will have to answer a variety of questions ranging from data handling to addition to the orientation of shapes and working out a pattern of numbers. Here the test is called 'mathematics' – and yet it also tests for numeracy!

Think about the sorts of things you use numeracy for in your everyday life and how often.

What is taught as 'mathematics'?

The National Curriculum sets out the statutory entitlement to learning for school-aged children. It determines what should be taught as mathematics and breaks this down into attainment targets for learning and levels to measure the learning against. Within this framework, schools must choose how to plan and organize their teaching and learning to ensure that children have access to their statutory entitlement to mathematics. Before 1999 there was no requirement to teach mathematics every day, as long as the National Curriculum was being covered.

After a four-year research project addressing the underachievement of children in mathematics compared to their European peers, the National Numeracy Strategy Framework for teaching mathematics was launched in primary schools in 1999 and a year later for students aged 11–13 at secondary school. The Department for Education recommended that a dedicated mathematics lesson should be taught daily in primary schools. The length of the lesson was and is still dependent on the age and ability of the students being taught, and the content of the lesson. The lesson should draw on elements of new teaching and reflection, as well as practice, rehearsal and consolidation.

In September 2006 the revised edition of the Primary Framework for Mathematics was published. The new publication acknowledges that things have moved on since 1999 – when the Framework was originally launched very few classrooms had a computer and now schools have computer suites, readily available Internet access and interactive teaching whiteboards. More research and resources have been published to support and extend, challenge and enhance all aspects of learning for all pupils, such as making links to other subjects and encouraging different speaking and listening skills.

There have been many changes in how a mathematics lesson is supported. In 1999 there were far fewer teaching assistants (TAs) employed in our schools and initially many were employed to support literacy – possibly as the literacy strategy came out one year before the numeracy one and possibly because without the skills to read and write most other subjects are affected.

Although this is changing, there are still more TAs supporting literacy and literacy catch-up programmes than numeracy and Wave 2 and 3 provision (see Chapter 5 for more details on intervention programmes in mathematics), but whether you are working in numeracy or literacy, you are still part of a team to support children's learning.

So what is your role within the lesson?

The role of the TA in supporting numeracy/mathematics often varies from child to child, class to class and school to school. You may be involved in preparing resources before or during the lesson, running intervention lessons or working alongside a child on their designated activity – for example, helping them to count backwards or complete a set of calculations. The lesson will have objectives set, often from the National Numeracy Strategy Framework, and the tasks are likely to extend, allow practice or consolidate that planned intention.

Mathematics planning from the Framework will draw from seven strands. They are listed below.

Using and applying mathematics

Children learn to solve problems that may involve money, measures or just numbers. For example, a carton of orange juice costs 30p. A multipack of four cartons costs £1. How much do you save by buying the multipack?

Your role might involve reading the problem, role-playing it or breaking it down into stages.

Counting and understanding number

You might be supporting children with counting on and back, understanding place value, percentages, fractions and decimals.

For example, you could play the following game and ask the children to read the place value of the created number. The game board below can be simplified to include tens and units only or extended to thousands, hundreds, tens and units or even decimals. The objective of the game is to make the highest possible number from the number displayed when you roll a dice. So, player A rolls the dice. He/she must then write the number under the column headings to represent the highest number he/she can make. So, for example, if a 3 is rolled, it can be entered as either 300, or 30 or 3. Player B has a go, and so on.

	Hundreds	Tens	Ones
Player A			
Player B			

Knowing and using number facts

These objectives are concerned with children learning the pairs of numbers to make 10 and then 20, and with learning the times tables.

For example, counting up and back in multiples and linking to the division facts:

$$0 \div 6 = 0$$
$$6 \div 6 = 1$$

$$12 \div 6 = 2$$
$$18 \div 6 = 3$$
$$24 \div 6 = 4$$
$$30 \div 6 = 5$$

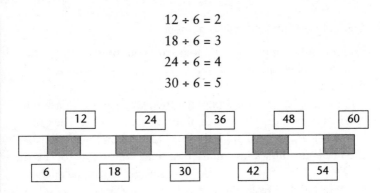

Your role might be to show the demarcated stick (often called a counting stick) and place sticky notes marked with the correct multiple of 6 (6, 12, 18 . . .) to act as a visual prop.

Calculating

Children learn to identify when to work out a calculation mentally, using a familiar written method or using a calculator.

For example, which of the following would you do in your head, on a calculator, jotting parts of the calculation down while doing the majority in your head, or using a reliable method?

$$5 + 2$$
$$3543646 \div 345$$
$$623 - 451$$
$$73 \times 4$$

You may be supporting children in estimating or working out the calculation and recognizing an appropriate method to use.

Understanding shape

Children are taught how to recognize and name shapes and properties of shapes and understand symmetry, angles and direction.

For example:

What shapes can you make with two cuts?

How many different regions can you make with four cuts?

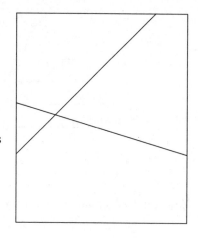

There are many ways this activity can be supported. The square could be cut out and children could draw the lines with rulers or actually make the cuts with scissors, or alternatively the square could be made from plasticine and the cuts made into it.

Measuring

Children learn about mass (weight), capacity and length. For example, you may be asked to support lessons where children are measuring and comparing the lengths of the infant and junior playgrounds.

Handling data

Children learn to classify, sort and organize a set of objects or numbers, then present their findings in a bar chart, pictogram, pie chart or table.

For example, which bus travelled most frequently along Dartmouth Road between 8am and 9am on 10 September?

Bus number
122
176
185
12
7
53

You could ask children what they could do to find the answer.

Blocks of work

Each term the children are taught five blocks of work. Each block of work contains elements from the 'Using and applying mathematics' strand and one or two other strands. For example, Block A contains counting and place value, calculating as well as using and applying objectives.

The same block of work is visited each term with an increase in complexity each time.

The new Framework continues to follow the statutory programmes of study set out in the National Curriculum.

The Early Years Foundation Stage curriculum

The 2006 Childcare Act legislated for a single framework for children from birth to five years old and this will be statutory from 2008.

The Early Years Foundation Stage is broken into six areas of learning, the problem-solving, reasoning and numeracy strand being mathematics specific. Mathematics learning includes sorting, matching, counting, working with shapes, numbers, spaces and measures, as well as making connections and seeking patterns and relationships.

Looking at the levels of attainment

As described in the statutory National Curriculum and defined in the 1996 Education Act, an attainment target sets out the knowledge, skills and understanding that pupils of different abilities and maturities are expected to have by the end of each Key Stage. In the National Curriculum the levels range from level 1 to level 8 in:

- Using and applying mathematics
- Number and algebra
- Shape, space and measures
- Handling data.

Children take statutory assessment tests at the end of Key Stages. These tests are assessed at the National Curriculum levels:

End of Key Stage	Year group	Age	Expected level
1	2	6–7	2
2	6	10–11	4
3	9	13–14	5

The levels of attainment for the end of each year are ambitious, pitched to ensure children reach the expected level 4 at the end of primary school.

The yearly teaching programmes therefore correspond to the following levels:

Year 1 objectives – level 1
Year 2 objectives – level 2
Year 3 objectives – level 3
Year 4 objectives – consolidation of level 3 and a start at level 4
Year 5 objectives – level 4
Year 6 objectives – consolidation of level 4 and a start at level 5.

Supporting children working below level 1

As TA you may be supporting children who are older than the Foundation Stage but who are working below level 1. The preliminary levels (P levels) have been written to offer further guidance.

The P levels break the curriculum down into a series of eight small steps (P1–8) leading to level 1 of the National Curriculum. They are useful for demonstrating the achievements of pupils with special educational needs and enable relevant targets to be set and attainment to be measured in more detail.

Think about how mathematics is taught in your school today compared to how it was taught in the past. Do you think it is broken down into logical areas?

2

Key mathematical skills

Why do some children struggle in mathematics? What key skills are missing?

Progression in mathematics

As children get older the complexity of the mathematics they learn increases. It progresses from learning simple number rhymes to counting whole numbers up to five, ten, one hundred, to counting in positive and negative numbers, decimals, fractions, and so on.

It is difficult for an adult to recall the steps of mathematical learning they underwent. The problem is that the progression is not linear – there are so many different aspects of mathematics – but progression can only be achieved if the basic skills are embedded first.

It may be that a child in Year 3 is identified as having special educational needs in mathematics – the missing pieces of information have been taught but they appear to be quickly lost. The problem may be that the objective needs to be tracked right back to the missing core skills. These are now discussed below.

Understanding and application of counting

Imagine for one minute what it was like to count to ten for the first time. As an adult, the understanding that when you count up in ones each new number increases by one every time, that numbers go on for ever, that 14 is one more than 13 tends to be taken for granted. There are so many stages in the understanding of the number system that counting tends to be regarded as a simple activity – but have you tried to count up and back in steps of 17 starting at 950?

At an early stage children recognize that the names used for counting are 'number' words, i.e. one, two, three, and that there is an order to how we say these words. These words are associated with an amount. The counting of that amount can only begin when the child recognizes that to count they need to point at an object and verbalize the number word, then point at the next object and verbalize the next sequential number word, and so on. This is also referred to as one-to-one correspondence.

Cardinality is the skill that recognizes that the last number counted is the number of objects in that group – so if eight objects have been pointed to and counted, there is a total of eight objects. There may be difficulties if the objects are of different sizes or cannot be physically touched or seen – for example, counting the pebbles being dropped into a pot or the moving bubbles blowing in the wind. Consequently, children need regular practice in counting toys, pencils, beads, and so on.

Activity

Ask children to count images on wrapping paper – if this is suggested as an investigation, the children will need to practise their skills of counting in order to solve it. For example, how many stars are there? Are there more stars than spots? What is the most commonly occurring shape?

The more children count, the more they develop the concept that if something is added to the objects the number increases, and if taken away the amount decreases. This understanding will become essential to grasping what happens in an addition and subtraction calculation.

It is also the case that the more children count, the more they recognize an amount without having to actually count. Consider the last time you counted the spots on a domino or a dice. The familiarity of the spots in a regular, recognized formation has meant that over time you have learned to identify the amount without having to count the individual spots. This is an essential skill needed for estimating groups or numbers of images or objects.

Regular practice with counting gives children a sense of the relative position of numbers in the number system. The understanding that these words relate to amounts can then be used and applied.

Having a picture of ordered numbers in our head must be intrinsically linked to how those numbers are written.

Here are some activities to help children practise counting:

▪ Count up and back in twos, fives or tens, starting from any two-digit number.
▪ Count up and back crossing 100 or 1,000.
▪ Count up and back with a physical movement, such as a wave or clap, when counting a multiple of a stated number. For example, to highlight counting in steps of six: 1, 2, 3, 4, 5, 6 (wave), 7, 8, etc.
▪ Play Fizz Buzz when counting in steps of 3 and 5 – count up from 1 and when the counted numbers reach a multiple of 3, instead of saying that number, say 'fizz'. Instead of saying the multiple of 5, say 'buzz' and instead of saying the multiple of 3 and 5, say 'fizz buzz':
1, 2, fizz, 4, buzz, fizz, 7, 8, fizz, buzz, 11 . . .

Understanding and application of the position of numbers

Development in mathematics goes beyond counting to seeing a number as a whole, i.e. when thinking of 5, children need to move away from thinking of 5 as five ones to an idea of 5 as a whole. Knowing how big a number is allows us to grasp the place of that number within our number system, so we do need to understand counting and have a feel for numbers and their relative positions.

Grouping in multiples of 10 is also fundamental to our number system and crucial for understanding place value.

Memory and retention

Retention is the ability to be affected by what we experience, to receive and process it and be able to communicate about it – it is the source of true memory. To memorize something we often need prompts such as visual or manipulative resources – diagrams, pictures, models – which will help us recall it.

The problem with memorizing can be that children learn concepts through rules and procedures or by rote, so it becomes almost a mechanical knowledge. For example, many adults remember how to carry out decomposition (breaking numbers down to aid calculation) but may have learned the rules rather than understood the concept.

As TAs we want children to retain information through personal, multisensory experiences. Children will struggle to understand if they have no experience of concepts, cannot internalize or make connections.

Practising just one key piece of knowledge, such as $2 \times 10 = 20$, little and often, supports the long-term retention of information. If a child learns all the times tables without making connections to previous learned information this could become an exercise in memory skills rather than in understanding and retention.

So, these are the core skills children need in order to progress in mathematics. Those children who demonstrate that they have specific needs in mathematics which are often borne out through lower attainment may require an individual education plan (IEP) to be written – or if more than one child displays the same need, then a group education plan may be drawn up.

Do you support a child with an education plan – is that plan for mathematics or is mathematics part of an overall plan for learning?

Individual and group education plans

The purpose of education for all children is the same; the goals are the same. But the help that individual children need in progressing towards them will be different.

(The Warnock Report, 1978)

Individual education plans are not compulsory and are only one method of planning provision to support an individual's needs. They are likely to be reviewed as a multi-agency approach – involving child, teacher, inclusion manager, TA and parents. If the school organizes personal learning programmes for each child then it is unlikely that IEPs will be written to record achievements.

Traditionally, many individual or group education plans highlighted targets for literacy or behaviour management, but often a child who struggled with reading and writing was likely also to struggle with reading and writing numbers. Over the last five years there has been more and more research on diagnosis and support for pupils demonstrating problems with numbers, and as a result school IEPs now reflect these special needs in mathematics. Also, there has been an increase in written targets for less specific needs – for those children who fall significantly behind their year group peers.

As a TA supporting mathematics, it could be that you will be supporting a written provision plan or map and preparing feedback on progress.

A Year 1 child's individual education plan may look like that shown in Table 2.1.

Table 2.1. Example of an individual education plan

Target	Additional provision	Success criteria	Evidence of success criteria
To write 9 correctly		Written 80%+ correctly in workbook	3/1/07 – on wipeable board for presenting answer 3/1/07 – workbook 10/1/07 – workbook 11/1/07 – verbally explained to TA how to form 9 correctly
To count the teens numbers in order	TA during mathematics lesson	Verbal, with confidence forwards and eventually backwards	7/1/07 – counted 11,12, 13, 14, then confused 8/1/07 – lack of confidence of order after 13. Does not recognize the 'thir' in 13 or 'fif' in 15
Bridge 19 to 20	TA during mathematics lesson	Verbal, with confidence with and without a number line	

Ideas for activities

Try some of these ideas for activities to probe understanding of counting, ordering, comparing and describing numbers. They are aimed at supporting Year 1 or 2 children who may be working with an education plan.

) objects

ld to collect favourite things from around the class-
oring them back and count them. Next ask the child

to put one away at a time. The child counts each 'new' reduced amount.

This could be extended to . . .

Ask the child to help unpack a bag of mixed items collected from around the classroom, counting the number of items from the bag. Your child recounts when putting items away. Ask questions such as, 'Are you sure there are six pencil sharpeners? Please check again.'

And then . . .

Ask the child to check that there is the correct number of items in a packet with a stated amount; for example, if the label says 30 pens, ask the child to check.

Reading numbers 1 to 10

Ask the child to identify numbers around the school – the clock, on the register, the school telephone number. The child is likely to say 'eight nine' for 89 as they identify each digit in the number.

Saying which number is larger/smaller, more/less

Write down 5 then 7 and ask which number is the larger/ smaller. If the child is not sure this is because they do not recognize the digit. Ask whether they would like 5 or 7 cakes and why? They may say that they would like 7 because it is 'more' or the 'largest amount'.

Can you think of some other ways children can practise counting and ordering? Try to use everyday objects that are familiar to the children and which may be particularly relevant to them – for example, coloured baubles on the school Christmas tree.

3

Working with the teacher

Roles and responsibilities within the mathematics lesson change depending on the year group and, often, the teacher. The teacher directs your role within the lesson. The Training and Development Agency (TDA) is now ensuring that all trainee teachers study modules on effective ways of working with additional adults within the classroom, and newly qualified teachers often receive this training as part of their local authority induction programme.

Your role in the mathematics lesson

Depending on your job description your main role and purpose in the mathematics lesson is to support teaching and learning. Supporting teaching might mean assisting with resources, 'teaching' a small group of children or managing the class to 'free' the teacher to teach small groups. Working with a group of children on an activity, taking a child out to practise the times tables or breaking down an objective into small achievable steps are all examples of supporting learning within the mathematics lesson.

So, during the mathematics lesson you are likely to be:

- working with an individual pupil
- working with a group or a group containing that individual child
- moving around the class supporting individuals
- working with a group in or out of the classroom.

The mental and oral part of the lesson

The purpose of the five- or ten-minute mental and oral section is to consolidate and practise those objectives previously taught. Key skills such as counting, recognizing place value, times tables and recall of number bonds are often revisited during this section of the lesson.

There is no requirement to start every lesson with a mental or oral activity. For example, if the teacher has planned a long problem-solving lesson then it may not be appropriate to have consolidation work as well. Similarly, if teaching something new the teacher may choose to start the lesson with the main teaching and use the end of the lesson or another time during the day for practice.

You are likely to be directed to work with those children whose abilities exceed the majority of the class and require extension, or those who require a simplification of the objective. You may be asked to work with children working way below their chronological years – this may be outside the classroom or sitting away from the rest of the class.

Examples of when the child or children might work outside the class:

- The class is practising ordering decimals to three decimal places – one group is working on recognizing decimals and the difference in place value before and after the decimal point.
- The class is practising the eight-times table. Child A practises counting on from and back to 8 from any given multiple of 8.
- The class is counting from 0 to 20. Child B counts on and back in different steps or counts on and back from any given number, e.g. 76 bridging 100.

Some teachers organize this practice part of the lesson with the children on the carpet, others ask children to remain at their desks. Whatever the organization, you will need to be positioned close to the child/group being supported. This proximity enables quiet discussion between you and the child without disturbing the concentration of the rest of the class. Speaking and listening skills between you and the child might include:

- the teacher's questions being rephrased
- prompts to remain on task
- answers from the child who lacks confidence to offer solutions in front of the class
- slowing the pace of the questions being asked
- offering visual or kinaesthetic (requiring active involvement) resources to aid response.

The main part of the lesson

The teacher will teach new learning by modelling, explaining, illustrating and demonstrating particular aspects of the objective. Again, while the teacher is teaching, you may be supporting a group of children with related questioning or resources, or breaking down the objective and teaching it at a slower pace.

The teacher will then instruct the children to complete a task linked to that learning intention. The children may work alone or in ability or mixed ability pairs or groups; whatever the organization, you will be supporting specific, identified children with their learning. It may be that you always work with the same group, where the learning is broken down into small steps.

It may be that for one reason or another (incident at break, urgent request by another teacher, first-aid, and so on) you have missed the introduction to the lesson. In order to know what mathematics needs to be supported during the main part, and if plans are not available, ask children to explain the task and the objective. Use generic questions such as:

- What are you learning today?
- How did the teacher explain x?
- Can you explain that in another way?
- How did the use of the number line/interactive whiteboard/100 square help you understand x?
- Would you like to use the same equipment?
- What words do you know about x?

Table 3.1 is an example of a support timetable, where the teacher has adult support in every mathematics lesson.

Table 3.1. Example of a support timetable

Ability	More able	Able	Focus group/ springboard group	Special needs
Monday	Independent work	Teacher focus 1	Teacher focus 2	Teaching assistant
Tuesday	Teacher focus 2	Independent work	Teaching assistant	Teacher focus 1
Wednesday	Teacher focus 1	Teacher focus 2	Teaching assistant	Independent work
Thursday	Independent work	Teaching assistant	Teacher focus 1	Teacher focus 2
Friday	Teacher focus 2	Teacher focus 1	Independent work	Teaching assistant

Terms used in the timetable:

- Focus group – the group of children whose attainment is just below that required for the year group, but not significantly so.
- Teacher focus 1 – the teacher works with this group for the majority of the lesson.

■ Teacher focus 2 – the teacher spends five minutes with this group to ensure that they are on task and understand the activity.

This timetable illustrates the range of support children in each ability group receive over the week – each group must also work independently of adult focus too. Becoming over-reliant on an adult explaining instructions or dependent on one-to-one attention will not help children to take responsibility for their own learning. It is all too common to see an adult talk through and demonstrate every step of the learning processes with the result that the skills are not transferred to the next lesson and the teacher or TA feels as if they are back at 'stage 1'.

During this part of the lesson, the support will be to:

■ prompt the learning by asking children to explain what they are doing and therefore learning
■ ask questions that will focus the thinking process
■ get children to explain instructions and clarify the task
■ demonstrate the main teaching again, using the same or different resources
■ manage any social aspects to the task, for example turn-taking in a game, and ensure on-task behaviour
■ manage and organize resources needed for the task
■ mentally assess the child's progress against the learning intention
■ answer any questions posed and clarify aspects of the teaching that weren't understood
■ prepare children for a presentation in the plenary.

Think about your own timetable for supporting children in mathematics lessons. Do you feel that there is a good balance between support and independent learning?

The plenary

The purpose of the plenary is to recap on the learning and provide time and opportunity for self- and class reflection. During the plenary children can measure their successes against the learning intention and you, the TA, can ascertain whether the child's self-evaluation is reasonable. Evidence can be gathered on the child's progress and the information can be used later for record-keeping.

It is also a time to reteach the objective if the teacher feels the majority of the class did not understand, or extend the objective and pave the way to future learning and the next lesson if the lesson was successful. Games may be played or questions asked to further assess children's learning.

Again, your role as TA in the plenary is similar to that in the mental and oral starter. Towards the end of the lesson there may also be opportunity to give brief, verbal feedback to the teacher or class on the learning of specific children or groups of children.

Think about some of the mathematics lessons you have observed or helped with. Can you identify the different stages and the purpose of each part?

Using the teacher's planning

Most schools provide TAs with access to the weekly planning for each class they support. The level of involvement in the planning stage varies from school to school. In the schools questioned by the National Teacher Research Panel, TAs regularly attended planning meetings on a voluntary basis or during assembly set time aside for discussions with teachers.

The detail of the role of the TA may vary with each lesson plan. Table 3.2 on page 28 shows an example of a Year 1 plan where the children are studying the language of capacity: full, empty and half-full. The role of the TA is shown for different parts of the lesson, and information on the group or individual to be supported is given.

The key information you need to obtain from the planning includes:

- the lesson's learning objectives – both the mental and oral starter and the main objective
- the key vocabulary to be stressed
- how the main objective is to be taught/illustrated/modelled – this is always useful if you need to repeat it when working with a group who have failed to understand the first explanation
- who you are supporting
- what you are supporting with – i.e. the differentiated task
- when you can feedback – verbally or as jotted notes.

How involved with planning are you? Do you have established planning meetings with your teacher?

Assessing pupils' learning

You may be involved with different types and levels of assessment. Summative assessment 'sums up' what the children have achieved and this is evident with end-of-year test results such as those from the Qualifications and Curriculum Authority (QCA) or Statutory Assessment Tasks (SATs). This form of assessment often tells you little more than that the child achieved a level 2A at the end of Year 3 – the results then need to be analysed by the teacher to be of use when supporting

Table 3.2. Key information

End of block/week theme: understanding capacity

Vocab: TA to circulate among mixed ability children asking them to identify full, empty, half-full

Mental/oral starter			Main teaching activity			
Objective(s)	Activity(s)	Objective(s)	Main teaching focus	TA role	Differentiated activities	
Count back in ones TA with Red Group with number track.	Sing 'Ten Green Bottles'. Use a number line, count back from 30. Ask children to clap while counting.	To understand and use the vocabulary related to capacity.	To demonstrate the language of full, empty and half-full. Demonstrate with different containers – 2 litre coke bottles, 50ml bottle. Half looks different in different containers. Which one holds most/least? Use a variety of sizes of bottles and demonstrate which is full, empty and half-full.	TA to support Blue Group with the language.	Mixed ability, children to rotate. Rice, sand, water. Use different containers, such as shampoo bottles. Children to demonstrate full, empty and half-full. Work as a group and each say the vocabulary.	

planning and differentiated work for children. As TA you may be involved with reading questions or invigilating in examinations in Key Stages 2 or 3. It is also possible that you may be asked to mark the tests using the QCA mark scheme guidance.

You are also likely to be assessing the children as you support them on a daily basis. This is known as formative assessment. Day-to-day assessment happens when you focus your attention on particular children each day and make a judgement on their understanding of the objectives. This may be through observation, marking or questioning during the lesson. The learning intention or objective needs to be explicit so that children know what they have learned rather than the activity they have done. At the beginning of the lesson, share with children in your group what they are going to learn and reflect on their successes in doing so at the end.

Here are some questions you could use to prompt the children to evaluate their own learning:

- What did you find easy about learning to . . . ?
- What are you most pleased with about learning to . . . ?
- What really made you think while you were learning to . . . ?
- What helped you when something got tricky?
- How would you do things differently next time, now you know what you know?
- What do you need more help with?
- What can you do now that you couldn't do before?
- What have you learned that is new about . . . ?
- How do you think we can use what we have learned today and in the future?
- How would you teach this objective to another group?

If you are using this form of assessment while working with a group, it's a good idea to jot down assessment comments on the children's learning against the intended objective. A proforma such as the one below may be helpful. It could also act as an effective feedback sheet too.

Maths group assessment/progress sheet

Class: 4 *Date:* 18 April *Objective:* to count on and back in ones from any given two-digit number.

Names	Comments
Ella	Counted on in ones from 1–19. She said 'twenteen' not 'twenty'. Needed to use 100 square to count back in ones
Oliver	Counted on in ones from 1–50. Counted back in ones but needed reminding when crossing from 20 back to 19
Anna	No support needed. Achieved

The notes sheet might look like this for a class of 30. Comments need to be informative but brief – if a child has not been able to meet the success criteria of the objective then which part have they not met? Of course, there will be some children for whom this level of assessment is unnecessary, as summative assessment or previous assessment states that the child is likely to exceed the objective or fail to meet it entirely.

Ongoing day-to-day assessment

This week children will be assessed for: Reading whole numbers to 1,000 and recognizing place value.

Questions targeted for:	Comment
Mohammed	Read 111 as one, one, one and struggled to recognize the difference between 100 and 10
Jack	Needed to be reminded of place value so used Base 10 equipment
Claire	Could read 356, 2,435, 33, 706 correctly.
Nathan	Read 51 as 15 and 71 as 17 – will need to use Base 10 in group work

Marking pupils' work

Traditionally, marking has tended to focus on:

- presentation, e.g. title and date, neatness
- surface features, e.g. digit in each box
- quantity
- the amount of effort involved – 'You worked hard here.'

Effective feedback to both child and teacher may be through oral, written or pictorial marking against the child's work. Oral feedback is potentially the most personal and effective as you can have a dialogue about the work with the child. However, this is not always possible in a busy classroom, so successful written marking focuses on the qualities of the children's work, if possible comparing it to previous work, stating what is good about it and specific ways in which it could be improved. Feedback is always related to the learning intention, and children must be clear about what success of that learning intention looks like.

So, comments could be:

'Great. You are beginning to use the grid method to help you to multiply. Look at the improvement since 13 December – well done, Jane.'

'Remember you can partition in lots of ways.'

Marking in this way may take more time than the simple 'Well done', but marking just a quarter of work like this is more effective than spending time making marks purely as a 'paper and pencil' exercise.

Many children compare marks and strive for a sticker. As a generalization, when stickers are used they tend to be given to the less able children, especially those who usually disrupt the lesson but have remained on task. If stickers are to be used, make a note of who has been given one and distribute them fairly to all children in the group or class; for some children who always work hard, never getting a sticker may deter them from doing the best they can do in the future.

Ways of feeding back to the teacher

Due to timetabling restraints it is often difficult for the TA to have a detailed conversation with the teacher at the end of the lesson, so written notes provide this link.

Any written notes on sheets, in books or as jotted notes in a planning file/diary provide invaluable insights into pupils' progress. Informative comments made as part of the marking process also provide levels of ongoing feedback. The intention is to aid further planning and differentiation if needed.

Comments should not be time-consuming to write. They could be jotted down when children are working or engaged in the plenary. They could look like this:

Red Group. *Class:* 2. *Date:* 14/9/07

Name:	Today's learning objective: order whole numbers to 100
Jane	Ordered all correctly
James	Read 71 as 17. Was confused when ordering numbers beyond 50 – more work needed on reading and writing numbers to 50
Janet	Worked with Jane – ordered correctly
Jamel	Could recognize when ordered smallest to largest and vice versa – extension needed
Josh	Needed support of 100 square – struggled to identify place value of tens when ordering
Jake	Ordered correctly

You could consider using a notebook to record pupils' progress and for two-way communication with the teacher.

Do you make notes like this for the teacher? Could you improve on your communication systems?

4

The effective use of resources

There are so many mathematical resources in a school, but how effectively are they being used to support mathematical learning? The more children play with a resource, use it, see it, the more they begin to internalize their understanding of the value of each digit in a number.

If you enter many Foundation Stage classrooms there will be an array of different equipment, from plastic bears for comparing, to coloured animals for counting, and beads for sequencing. As children get older there tends to be less equipment available for use in a mathematics lesson. This chapter looks at the range of resources and at how, if you use them regularly with the pupils you support, they can become a tool for learning, irrespective of age.

A feel for number – the 'fiveness' of five

Numicon™ or Cuisenaire rods are coloured rods. They come in a variety of different lengths and are used to give a visual representation of numbers. These resources show whole numbers in relation to others. They give the image of 5 as one more than 4, as well as a distinct pattern in its own right. Children are drawn to finding 'how many', without counting. When ordered, the staircase pattern provides a visual association of the next number and one more/one less.

The Numicon™ or Cuisenaire sets support the understanding of numbers and calculations by emphasizing the wholeness

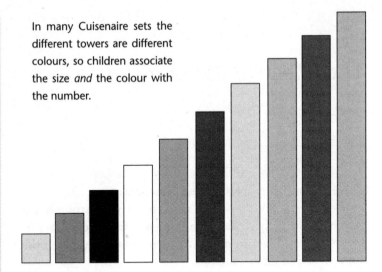

In many Cuisenaire sets the different towers are different colours, so children associate the size *and* the colour with the number.

of numbers. If children are encouraged to approach calculation through an experience of counting then they may work out 3 + 2 by counting out three then counting out two and counting altogether, often starting back at one, (which we don't want in later life but praise them for when younger). If we transfer this idea to 43 + 12, we would hope that they do not count out 43, then count out 12, then count altogether.

These resources also demonstrate the importance of equivalents/equals, i.e. 3 and 2 are equivalent to 5 – by lining up the whole number representations and proving that the 3 and 2 weigh the same and are the same length as the 5.

Recognition of the written number

Children need to see the written number regularly, recognize its shape, describe it, copy it, internalize it and see it in their head – all this alongside the associated quantity. Here are some ideas to help them with this:

- Bury a wooden or plastic written digit in some sand or in a bag – when children discover the number they must say it and write it down.
- Place the digit behind a screen and get the children to work out the number from a small revealed part.
- Fish for the digit in water.

Find as many different ways as you can for children to have to deduce what the digit is. If you ask questions such as, 'Is it a curved number?' the children can work out what it could be and dismiss what it is not.

Children need to see written numerals regularly – on a number track, on number tiles, in a 100 square, and so on – and to be asked questions about the position of the number in relation to others.

Activities might include:

This is a 100 square

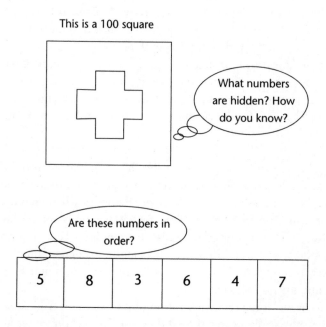

What numbers are hidden? How do you know?

Are these numbers in order?

| 5 | 8 | 3 | 6 | 4 | 7 |

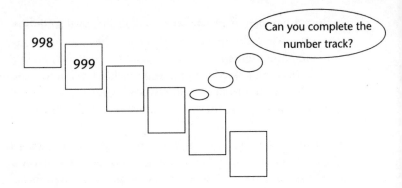

There are many materials on the market that you could use to show the position of numbers and number sequences.

Number tracks and squares

The 100 square is one of the most common visual images found in the classroom. It compactly displays 100 numbers and acts as a tool for counting up and back in ones or tens or different sized multiples and describing the pattern.

It demonstrates cardinality – the 37th square is marked with 37 – and the significance of the multiples of 10 is clear because when you reach 10, 20, 30, and so on, you must start a new line. The grid can be cut into strips and reordered to form a line of 100 numbers.

But if the 100 square is in almost every classroom, then why do children still struggle to transfer this visual image into their heads? For some children it may be that there are too many numbers in a relatively small shape, therefore when reading a line at a time from left to right they may simply miss a line. Also, having continuous access to the first 100 counting numbers, some children may struggle to recognize numbers over 100 – where is 101? – and the notion that numbers are continuous is removed.

In terms of the relative position of number, on a 100 square 31 is physically nearer the 40 than the 30 – again presenting confusion if transferring to a blank number line or if rounding the number down.

So the 100 square has its advantages and disadvantages, but it does need to be viewed in conjunction with a 100 line. This is more difficult to display in a classroom because of its sheer length and the fact that the written number falls at the end of a line rather than in a whole square. A number line may look very similar to a ruler.

On some number lines the decades of numbers are marked with alternating colours – red/blue, red/blue. The emphasis here is on the importance of the 'tens' numbers. Children can then move from this horizontal image of numbers using a line to doing calculations. The disadvantage, like the 100 square, is that manufactured materials still only show the first 100 counting numbers.

Again, the more children have access to the number line or track the more it becomes internalized and part of their long-term memory. Having an understanding of 30 in relation to 40 or 23 is an essential skill when it comes to calculation. The strategy used to subtract 39 from 41 may be different if you are confident and secure of the relative position of those numbers as opposed to dismissing the value of the numbers and opting for a 'take away' calculation.

For example, a visual image for 41 – 39 =

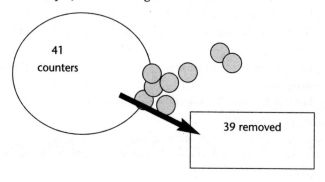

41 counters

39 removed

i.e. 41 take away 1, 2, 3, 4 . . . and 39

Or using a number line for 39, counting on to 40 and on to 41.

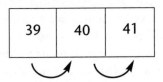

A blank or empty number line

The visual number line or track becomes a tool to apply to calculations – the children can transfer the relative position of a number to a blank or empty number line or bead string. The bead string acts as a 'transference' resource from the numbered lines or tracks to individual unnumbered beads – and at any stage, the child can count the beads and check their calculations.

Bead strings are a relatively inexpensive resource. They contain 10 or 100 beads along a string, demarcating each tens number with different or alternating colours, such as white and red. The beads can be pulled or slid across.

If you are using a bead string with your pupils, try asking some of these questions:

- If 0 is one end and 100 is the other, roughly where is 34?
- If 0 is one end and 1 is the other, what is each bead worth? (0.01)
- Can you find 42? How many tens did you pull across, how many ones?
- How many would you add to 32 to show 47? 55?

As well as a resource for recognizing the position of numbers, the bead string can be used to aid calculation, i.e. finding the difference between two numbers, adding on, counting up and back in sets of multiples. Some questions you could ask include:

- If I went to the shop with £1 and spent 43p, how much change would I get?
- What is missing . . . 6.7 + ? = 10
- Can you count up and back in multiples of 10?

By moving away from the number track or beads and on to an empty number line you can help children to build a mental picture of the position of numbers and how this knowledge can be applied to calculations. It requires only a piece of paper and a pencil and children can decide the numbers they mark on.

For example: 423 – 38 =

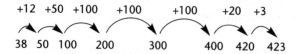

An understanding of place value

Grouping in multiples of ten is fundamental to our number system. Resources such as Numicon™, Dienes/Base 10, and Cuisenaire rods, or bundles of straws grouped in bunches of tens and hundreds which highlight the significance of tens with different colours or shapes, are crucial tools for understanding place value. Children can feel the difference in size and there-fore the value of 10 as opposed to 1, and 100 as opposed to 10.

Children need to see and feel the difference in size to under-stand the place value of 1,111. A problem with only using

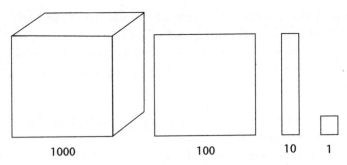

place value charts/cards is that they are only numerals. You cannot feel the 'eighteenness' of 18, only see the digits.

Try these activities to support an understanding of place value:

- Turn over a two- or three-digit card, for example 58. Ask pairs to say the number, and then select the appropriate Base 10 resource to make the number. Children then record the visual representation (see opposite).
- Alternatively, start with the visual representation and work back to the written form.

Ask children the following questions:

- Can you make and display 58 with straws?
- How would you make 208? What is the place value of each digit?
- What changes when you add one to 19?
- Explain what happens when 10 is added to/subtracted from 23?

Making a key resources 'kit'

Irrespective of the year group that you are supporting, have a plastic wallet, envelope or bag of key resources that can be carried from lesson to lesson and group to group. This means you won't be relying on the equipment being in place and

Numerals	How we say the number	Visual
58	Fifty-eight	
112	One hundred and twelve	

accessible in each classroom. Your resource kit can then be personalized to suit the interests of the child/group you are supporting. You could include, for example, wrapping paper for counting bicycles that may be more motivating than, say, stars; counters in the shape of animals as opposed to flat counters; a non-age-specific number track rather than one clearly designed for the early years, and so on.

The kit might change over the year to reflect the different strands of mathematics being studied, but it will always be useful to contain those resources that support the basic skills, such as:

- A selection of Base 10 equipment – for place value.
- One set of Cuisenaire rods – for wholeness of numbers and calculating.
- Dice – for recognition of amounts.
- Counters or interlocking cubes – for counting.
- Number lines – for calculating and position of number.
- Number tracks such as the 100 square – for position of number and patterns.
- Bead strings – for position of number and calculating.

Using ICT to motivate learners

For many children, ICT can provide the motivation for learning and/or consolidating particular concepts, such as the relationship between numbers and the carrying out of mental addition and subtraction, skills in problem-solving and the rapid recall of multiplication and division facts.

The ICT intended for use within the daily mathematics lesson needs to be readily available, easy to use and should suit any classroom situation. Ultimately it must enhance the mathematics objective being taught and stimulate all children within the class to want to participate in the lesson – if it doesn't, then its use is unnecessary. An interactive whiteboard needs to be exactly that – interactive!

The use of calculators in mathematics lessons has been the cause of much debate over the years. Advocates for their use make claims that the technology speeds up the calculation process so children can develop higher order thinking and reasoning. Others claim that an over reliance on a 'machine' can weaken mathematical thinking.

The National Numeracy Strategy gives guidance for schools on the use of calculators. In Key Stage 2, when children have acquired a range of number skills, calculators are used to aid more complex problem solving and calculations. In all year groups, the calculator provides the TA with another visual tool for teaching concepts and can be used as a motivating tool for learners.

Try some of these activities using a calculator with the children you support to consolidate their understanding of number.

- Activity 1 – on the calculator put in 6,789. Ask the children whether they can read the number, how they would make the 6 disappear, what key sequence would need to be entered, and so on. Repeat, subtracting the other numbers until the screen returns to 0.

- Activity 2 – on the calculator enter 7 and keep multiplying by 10. Ask pupils to explain what is happening to the original 7 and illustrate that the 7 is getting 10 times bigger and the 7 digit moves to the left. Challenge children who may say they add the zero to the end of the 7.

- Activity 3 – write out the numbers below on the board. Ask children to imagine they represent plots of land with potatoes. Ask questions such as:

  - Which four plots of land give approximately 1,000 potatoes? (For example, the plots with 332, 81, 25 and 575 will provide 1,013 potatoes.)
  - Which three adjoining plots give the most potatoes? (644, 538 and 630)
  - Which two plots add together to make 637 potatoes? (469 and 168)

276	380	81	332
341	644	538	630
575	25	189	93
469	168	438	132

Children can use a calculator to add the three-digit numbers (they could also estimate or add the numbers mentally).

There is a wide range of maths-based computer software available on the market – some of the games and programs are for children, and others illustrate main teaching concepts. The teaching of ICT skills needs to happen in the ICT curriculum – and the children need to have the ICT skills to access the mathematics.

Written in 2000, programs such as these free downloadable resources from The Standards Site – www.standards.dfes.gov.uk – can enhance children's enjoyment of the subject as well as consolidating calculation and number recognition skills:

■ Activity 1 – the *Function Machine* program. First, illustrate how a function machine works with a box – put a card with the number 5 written on into the left side, shake the box, and pull out a card which shows number 11. Ask the children to guess what calculation is occurring 'in the box' to turn the 5 into 11. Repeat with another example, such as the card with 11 written on it, pulling out a card showing 17. Repeat until children recognize that the +6 function is being used. Now demonstrate the same concept with the computer program. Choose a rule but hide it, then ask for a number to be placed into the 'input' space, press 'activate' and watch the 'output'. Press 'reveal' to show the function.

■ Activity 2 – *Counter* illustrates counting in steps or multiples in whole and/or decimal numbers. Demonstrate on the slowest speed with a child deciding the start number and step size, then encourage the group to count on in that step or predict the number of the next step.

■ Activity 3 – *Play Train* is a program that illustrates the need for constant revision and practice of multiples and times tables. This program is used for a range of age groups from Years 1 to 6 to consolidate partitioning a number using multiples of 1 to 9. For example, 58 can be made up from $5 \times 6 = 30$ and $4 \times 7 = 28$.

Many schools now have ICT suites that can be used by different classes across the week. It may be that you, the TA, can take a group outside the lesson to the suite and access the wealth of motivating websites out there. Depending on the unit of work being studied, a search using a recognizable search engine will often bring up hundreds of pages that can be accessed for suitability prior to the lesson. Some useful ones are:

■ www.counton.org – this site is for primary and secondary aged children. Double click on 'Numberland'; this provides mathematical information as well as general information on selected numbers.

- www.nrich.maths.org.uk – this site demonstrates the wide range of problem-solving activities and investigations that promote children's questioning skills, trial and error methods, perseverance and strategies. The investigations can be printed off and children can work at them at their own pace. Many of the investigations are fairly simple to start with, with patterning and sequence skills that can be understood more clearly with the animated link.
- www.bbc.co.uk/jam – this is the 'digital brain' section of the BBC website and has interactive 'games' which progress in complexity, as well as problems to solve. For example, there is a rabbit that must move forwards and backwards along a number line collecting carrots, and a maze with doors that can only be entered if the squares are collected and rearranged appropriately.

Do you have access to an ICT suite in your school? Think about different ways you could use ICT to get children interested in mathematics. Could you research any new computer programs which might be useful?

5

Using intervention materials

What is differentiation?

Differentiation is about recognizing differences and distinguishing between them. In a classroom setting it is about improving access to learning by accounting for individual differences in learning style, interest, motivation and ability. By acknowledging and accounting for different needs, the aim for all those involved in education is to ensure that children work to their full potential and achieve success through sustained interest in the learning.

Differentiation needs to be pre-planned. It may be as part of the:

- teaching
- task
- response.

So, when as TA you are supporting an individual or a group identified for differentiated support, consider the following questions.

The teaching

How is the information and knowledge presented? Have you ensured that all children can see the board or interactive whiteboard and are they able to read it? If not, you need to read the information for them or break it down into smaller steps for learning.

Is the mode of presentation varied? How are you going to present information to children when working with them in a group? You will need to use a variety of methods, such as the interactive whiteboard, wipeable boards, books, artefacts and equipment.

Are the children clear about the learning intention and outcome? You need to explain the learning intention to them in child-friendly language, breaking the tasks down into manageable and achievable steps. For example, if the class objective is addition and subtraction of £ and p, this can be differentiated for less able learners as adding and subtracting multiples of 10p. It can also be simplified for one child as recognizing 1p and 2p.

Are resources easily available, so that movement and noise can be reduced? Ensure that you have a bag of resources that can be used when working with a group, and know where to find key equipment such as Base 10, counters or Cuisenaire rods in the classroom in which you are working.

The task

How are children asked to carry out a task? Ask children to repeat the instructions and, if necessary, demonstrate what they should do. Avoid repeating the instructions yourself, but simplify them by using diagrams, pictures or verbal clues.

Will children work in groups, as individuals or in pairs? Often when children are asked to work as a group, they do not – they work as six individuals sitting round a table. You will need to keep the group on task and praise them when they are working well together. Vary how children work – they will be less motivated if they always work in one way.

Problems can arise if the less able children are always grouped together as they are less likely to have a role model to show what effective learning looks like. They may coast along, devoid of challenge, lacking in collaborative learning or joint outcome. Your role as TA, therefore, will be to promote listening, value effort, not answers, and develop the attitude that 'no answer is a wrong answer'. You may provide a voice for this group, ensuring that the teacher acknowledges the answers and effort of pupils working in the group.

The response

Children of different abilities can be supported and/or challenged by how they respond, whether this is verbally, in writing or visually. In, for example, open-ended problem-solving activities, the level of response will vary in the complexity of the answer, reasoning and length. You may support the methods of recording such as pictures, flow charts, cartoons, neat work, ideas, jottings, large group work, photographs, and so on.

So, in general, you can improve children's access to the curriculum by differentiating according to:

- learning objective/aims of the lesson
- content
- presentation of the information
- breadth and depth of understanding
- level of maturity of response and confidence in oral work
- pace
- language
- resources
- form of adult-to-pupil or pupil-to-pupil interactions
- form of assessment
- teaching style
- classroom organisation.

Identifying specific learning difficulties in mathematics

Traditionally, children are identified as having specific educational needs in literacy, but you may be supporting children identified as having general needs that also affect their numeracy skills. Only in recent years have specific needs in mathematics been researched, and with this more children are being identified as having dyscalculia (difficulties with numbers). Read on to find out more about this need and others less specific to mathematics but affecting understanding and attainment.

Dyslexia and dyscalculia

Dyslexia is a difficulty concerning the processing of language, where children have problems in reading, spelling and/or writing. This may be accompanied by difficulties in number work, sequencing, motor skills and organizing and memorizing information.

Dyscalculia is like dyslexia but with numbers, and it affects the ability to acquire arithmetical skills. Children with dyscalculia lack an intuitive grasp of numbers, particularly when applied to time, money or measures.

If a child is dyslexic or dyscalculic, he/she may have always struggled with recognizing numbers (particularly if only presented on a 100 square where the numbers might seem to 'move about') and so over time has 'given up' or lacks the confidence to 'give it a go'. Much of your time may be spent encouraging, praising and celebrating small steps of success.

Dyslexic and dyscalculic children may struggle with maintaining the order for counting. Count aloud at the start of each group task and ask the child to join in when he/she is confident. Concentrate on the numbers in the number system, their position and value, and how the number is said.

Children need to become familiar with the language of mathematics. Activities during group work might include asking pairs of children to read a word from a card, say a definition and/or draw its meaning and then develop strategies that will help to remember it. Here are some examples you could model to start children off:

- 1ne, 2wo, 3hree, 4our, 5ive . . .
- Addddddding
- Sub – tracting
- Multi multi multiplying
- Div id in g

Make up sentences with the word in, role-play, discuss and analyse the language, and spend a bit of time each day on the vocabulary.

Children displaying dyscalculia may reverse their digits when writing. Depending on their age, ask children to practise writing digits in water on outside walls or on the side of a water tray, in paint or glue, on the interactive whiteboard or using different pens, pencils and crayons in their books.

Many dyslexic and dyscalculic children will find it difficult to organize their learning. Have the resources laid out in front of the child and, if necessary, store this equipment in an easily accessible and labelled bag. A number track rather than a number square may be easier to read and should be readily available. Dyscalculic children will have poor time-keeping skills, so count down to the end of the lesson every five minutes so that they will be able to complete their work. If possible, establish a 'benchmark' for what five minutes feels like – use a stop clock or timer set to five-minute intervals.

Use concrete materials to demonstrate what is happening with numbers. The interactive whiteboard provides opportunities for visual learners, but for many dyslexic children the understanding comes from tactile and kinaesthetic learning (learning through active involvement and experience). For example, use Base 10 equipment to highlight the differences in place value of the digits, and use pegboards or cut out rectangles from squared paper to show the order for a particular timetable. To understand the place value of 2,465, try using some of the mathematics resources to show it as in the diagram on page 54.

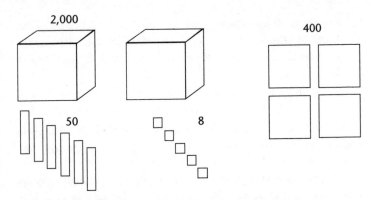

Or to demonstrate how the three-times table develops:

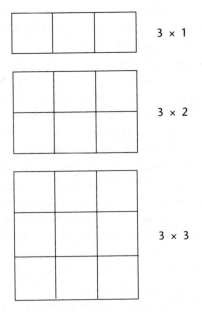

Dyslexic and dyscalculic children can struggle to learn and recall the times tables – this is often because they are viewed as unrelated facts. Start a child off by developing confidence and strategies to recall one fact – for example 3 × 1 – then move on to linking that known fact to 3 × 2 . . . and on to using doubling to 3 × 4 and 3 × 8. Over time the child then has a bank of known facts and strategies from which to derive new facts.

Often children will not learn facts if following someone else's rules or explanations. You will need to set time aside for children to make up their own rules to remember or 'internalize' what has been taught.

There are many resources where numbers appear in different ways and this may be confusing for children with dyslexia or dyscalculia. When there are lessons in which a protractor (reading angles using the left to right or right to left scale), thermometer (negative numbers), rulers or calculators are used, you will need to demonstrate how to use them before asking the children to find answers. Ask questions such as:

■ Who can find me 9 on a calculator? Draw the keys to the left, right, above and below.
■ What happens to the numbers below the 0 on a thermometer?
■ Can you demonstrate to the group how to use a protractor?
■ Can you read the scale on that bar chart? What is it going up in?
■ If you had to tell someone how to use a protractor, what would you say?

For all of us, it can be daunting to be asked to instantly recall a fact. When working with dyslexic children you have to consider their lack of confidence and remember that they are generally much slower to recall strategies or facts. Ensure that you build in 'thinking time' before asking for responses.

And use wipeable boards where children can write their responses. They may be more motivated to record their strategy if they know it can be rubbed out.

But remember, not all dyslexic or dyscalculic children have the same problems or indeed are supported with the same differentiated 'menu'.

Autistic spectrum disorder

There are varying degrees of autistic spectrum disorder (ASD). Children on the spectrum may show a tendency for repetition, a lack of communication or indifference to others, a lack of awareness of others around and an inability to play imaginatively. There can be language disorder, with poor attention/hyperactivity, unusual response to sensory stimuli, poor fine motor skills and difficulties with reading and number.

In terms of mathematics, children with ASD may have difficulties with counting on from different starting points. They may be unlikely to join in whole-class counting as they may repeat numbers or be disturbed by noise, so provide opportunities for them to count on their own. You may need to actually take the child out of class to count alone and away from distractions.

Avoid setting the mathematics in contexts. Some children will see no point in imaginative situations or in illustrations and may get bogged down in the imaginative part and miss the mathematics – for example, if you are going to be calculating time, use a concrete example such as a local bus timetable. Provide numbered cards lacking any illustration – if you show the number as four yachts, then the child may be preoccupied with the yachts.

Children with ASD will see little point in the need to explain answers, so avoid the 'how do you know' questions. Often marked work is ignored or seen as someone defacing the work, so try to avoid this but keep notes in a journal on the child's progress.

Pupils will need clear time guidelines as to how much work is expected and in what time. Some children with ASD become anxious as the lesson draws to a close, because they know the routine is about to change. Try to build in auditory and visual clues that the lesson is ending – for example, if you have a resource bag, make a point of saying, 'The lesson is finishing, we need to put away the resources.'

On the opposite side of the ability spectrum are those children who struggle with language and comprehension, but have extraordinary skills in mathematics, mental ability and memory. Take Daniel Tammet, who was described in an article in the *Guardian* in 2005: 'Tammet is calculating 377 multiplied by 795. Actually, he isn't "calculating": there is nothing conscious about what he is doing. He arrives at the answer instantly. Since his epileptic fit, he has been able to see numbers as shapes, colours and textures. The number two, for instance, is a motion, and five is a clap of thunder. "When I multiply numbers together, I see two shapes. The image starts to change and evolve, and a third shape emerges. That's the answer. It's mental imagery. It's like maths without having to think."'

These abilities are so extreme that it would be difficult for many of us to support a child such as Tammet's mathematics at that level. However, he or she would still require time cues, support for organization and much praise and encouragement.

Children with ASD often have special interests, such as cars or trains. Can you think of ways to use these interests when you are supporting learning in mathematics?

Published support/differentiated materials

The National Numeracy Strategy has described the differentiation of mathematics as 'waves of support'. Each wave of support must be based on clear assessment of the children's understanding tracked over the year. Wave 1 is the effective inclusion of all children in high quality teaching and learning.

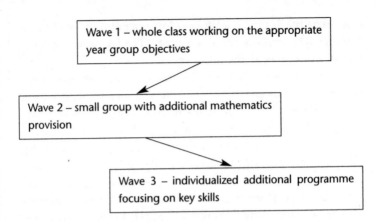

Wave 1 – whole class working on the appropriate year group objectives

Wave 2 – small group with additional mathematics provision

Wave 3 – individualized additional programme focusing on key skills

Headteachers, mathematics subject leaders, special needs/ inclusion coordinators and teachers will need to analyse the SATs and QCA data at the end of each year to decide what levels of differentiated provision will need to be set up for the start of the new year. You may be asked to deliver or support the delivery of some of this provision.

Intervention in the form of additional mathematics sessions, even for a limited period, has a beneficial impact on confidence, extending understanding and attainment. Many schools provide extra time for small groups to consolidate what has been taught in class or to follow an additional programme. Sessions are aimed at those pupils falling just below the expected National Curriculum levels for that year group, who, with targeting and support, can reach the expected levels of their peers.

The Springboard programme, first introduced into schools in 2000, is designed to help pupils in Years 3, 4, 5 and 7 who are falling a little behind in mathematics. The materials focus on key areas of number and target pupils' areas of weakness. They come with a video of clips of the lead lessons, showing how the materials can be broken down. The video looks at the objectives to be covered in the lessons, with links back and to the appropriate year group. The lessons are initially taught to a small group of children by a teacher. If necessary, additional support can be offered by a TA who will then work with the group for a 30-minute session.

These materials can provide some useful teaching strategies. However, if you are supporting children working significantly below their age-related attainment, you may need to use Wave 3 provisions.

Supporting low attainers using Wave 3 materials

The Wave 3 programme is focused on the teaching of key skills and tackling fundamental errors and misconceptions that are preventing progress. These children will have been identified through data, are likely to be on the special needs register or have missed a lot of schooling. They may have attended Wave 2 provision but it is deemed that this is not having the desired effect. Again, it is likely to be the special needs/inclusion coordinator who has timetabled this provision outside the daily mathematics lesson and it is likely to be delivered by you, the TA.

If you already work with children requiring this level of differentiation then you would not be surprised to see that the repetitive teaching focuses on:

- counting on and back
- ordering numbers
- partitioning and recombining
- addition and subtraction facts to 20
- understanding of addition, subtraction, division and multiplication
- problem-solving strategies.

Communication between you, the teacher and the special needs/inclusion coordinator is key, as is managing exit strategies for the child if they no longer need to be on the programme.

Supporting EAL learners

The mathematics lesson can be a confusing time for pupils who are learning English as an additional language. Imagine for a moment what it would feel like if you were asked to start counting in ones in Japanese – it would help if you could see the numbers and could hear or read the translation. For example:

1   Ichi
2   Ni
3   San
4   Shi
5   Go
6   Roku
7   Shichi
8   Hachi
9   Ku
10 Ju

Having a visual support such as a number line or track and pointing to the number when counting can help children with English as an additional language to keep up with the rest of the class. Over time they can begin to join in when they hear a word they recognize alongside the written numeral. When working with a group, repeat the sounds of numbers and refer to the written numeral as much as possible. Encourage children to join in, whether they are writing or saying numbers in English or another language.

These children need ways other than speaking to show their involvement in the lesson, so using resources – bead strings, fans, digit cards, etc. – for responding without saying the words will enable them to access the lesson. Have a set of resources available for children who are not confident enough to speak in the mental starter or plenary part of the lesson.

By using resources you can model the actual learning and illustrate concepts. The child can then use the equipment to repeat the concept and by doing so demonstrate some level of understanding.

If language is being used, allow thinking time to process that language – repeat questions, and repeat again. Provide illustrations alongside vocabulary, so that children start to pick up and use the correct mathematical words. The children can also write the word in their first language as a prompt, for example:

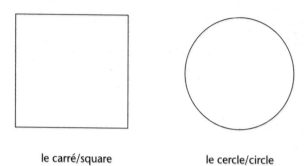

le carré/square   le cercle/circle

Consider the complexities of mathematical language. Words such as product, volume, table, difference, set, factor can mean different things in different contexts. And what about the prepositions – in, of, on – and the difficulties these can cause? Phrases such as 'find three-quarters of 16 cakes', or 'reduce by 5 cm' can be hard to grasp. The same preposition can signify different calculations, for example, 3 multiplied by 10, and 3 increased by 10. Now imagine trying to translate these.

By understanding just how complicated it is we can empathise with how children must feel learning the English number system for the first time. Build confidence, using praise at every opportunity.

When supporting children during the main lesson activity, consider positioning someone with good language abilities who is able to articulate their mathematical thinking clearly next to an EAL child. This supports peer working but also higher order thinking for the pupil who is peer tutoring and has to convey their thought processes for a problem without using language and is reliant on illustrations or calculations. Also, support different language levels by playing games with few verbal instructions.

Working with children who have different home languages may provide you with the opportunity to 'brush up' or learn a new language!

How many different languages do children in your school speak? Remember to treat the ability to speak another language as a gift.

6

The art of questioning –
speaking and listening

As adults we ascertain levels of understanding in mathematics by observation, marking work, listening and talking to children. You can often help to make ideas clearer by simply asking children to explain their answers and strategies.

For example, ask a child to explain their answer to the calculation $6.7 + ? = 10$. The child has recorded 4.3 in the missing box. He starts by explaining that he needed to add 0.3 to 0.7 to add on to the next whole number, that is 7. He then recognizes that if 4 were added on the answer would be 11. So the correct answer must be 3.3 and not 4.3. Only by explaining, and thus prompting the thought process again, did the child recognize and correct the error.

The importance of questioning

You can extend children's thinking in numeracy by asking questions throughout the lesson. By asking questions you are prompting their ideas and thoughts, often providing opportunities to self-reflect as well as developing skills for independent working and learning. For example, a boy in your group has been given the instructions to a task but he says he has forgotten and does not get started. It is easier to repeat the instructions but this is unlikely to develop his listening skills for next time. So for children that are stuck, try asking:

- Can you describe the problem in your own words?
- Can you describe what you have done so far?

- What did you do last time? What is the same/different this time?
- Is there something that you already know that might help?
- Could you try it with simpler/fewer numbers? Would a number line help?
- Would a picture or diagram help?
- Why not make a guess and check if it works?
- Have you compared your work with anyone else's?

You can also ask questions when pupils are starting a piece of work. The questions below are generic and could be used in most lessons. Only one or two need to be asked to extend children's thinking further.

- How are you going to tackle this?
- What information do you have/need?
- Which operation/s are you going to use?
- Will you do it mentally, with a pencil and paper, using a number line, or with a calculator? Why?
- What method are you going to use? Why?
- How are you going to record what you are doing?
- Can you estimate or predict what the answer will be?

To check progress while the children are working ask:

- Can you explain what you have done so far? What is the next step?
- Why did you decide to use that method?
- Can you think of another method that might have worked?
- Could there be a quicker way of doing this?
- What did you notice?
- Can you see a pattern or a rule?
- Do you think that this would work with other numbers?
- Have you thought of all the possibilities? How can you be certain?

At the end of the lesson ask:

- How did you get this answer?
- Can you describe your method/pattern/rule to the class/group and explain why it works?
- What could you try next?
- Would it work with different numbers?
- What if you had started with . . . rather than . . . ?
- What if you could only use . . . ?
- Is it a reasonable answer/result? What makes you say so?
- How did you check your answer?
- What have you learned or found out today?
- If you were doing it again, what would you do differently?
- What are the key points you need to remember?

The use of open and closed questions

Some questions are better than others at enabling teachers and TAs to assess children's understanding. Varying the way questions are asked can affect the answer that the pupil gives.

'Open' questions require the response to be more than a short or one-word answer. Look at these examples:

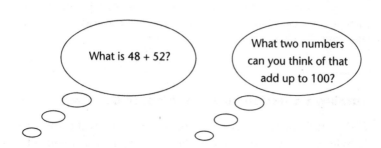

What is 48 + 52?

What two numbers can you think of that add up to 100?

The first question is closed – it allows you to assess a correct or incorrect answer. In the second example, the child may say 48 and 52, but the choice of numbers is personal. The open question encourages children to think in a different way.

Other examples of open and closed questions:

Closed	Open
Name the shape	Which shapes have four sides and four angles?
How many?	What different ways could you use to count these?
15 – 7 = ?	What two numbers have a difference of 8?
5p + 5p = ?	What coins add up to 10p?
An apple costs 12p and an orange costs 35p. How much do they cost altogether?	I spent 47p on an apple and an orange. What may each one have cost?

Turning a question into a problem to be solved

Let's return to the closed and open question in the speech bubbles above. If you now ask whether there are other pairs of numbers that total 100, the question has changed from being relatively quick to answer to an investigation that may take the whole lesson and requires far greater thinking.

By changing the wording slightly, the question becomes a problem that needs to be solved. It is likely to use the same mathematics, but it is the depth of understanding that is demonstrated.

Take the next example: When returning from an outing, the children are asked to count the number of houses along the street. Such a question involves the skills needed for counting. Now if we enrich that question we may say, 'Is there the same number of houses in all the roads leading to the school?'

Or we could ask, 'A boy is delivering free newspapers; he has 30 left in his bag. Will he have enough for every home on this street?'

In either of the above questions, there is so much more involved than just counting. To find the answer the children would have to demonstrate an understanding of counting, comparison and difference.

This type of question or problem is far more motivating and requires the children to use greater mathematical skills. So, consider reducing the number of questions you pose to children and extending the level of complexity by simply altering the wording.

Try making your own list of open questions to prompt extended mathematical thinking.

Using role play

Role play, all too often associated with Nursery or Reception classes, gives children the 'freedom' and opportunity to act out familiar and unfamiliar settings. By presenting a scene, such as a fruit shop or post office, you give children the opportunity to develop their understanding of real-life contexts using money, number, time and measures and to act out ideas, communicate reasoning and develop social skills. Having the confidence to share methods and ideas and discuss strategies lies at the heart of attempting much mathematics. Combining role play and mathematics is a practical, fun but fundamental way of introducing children to thinking through methods, strategies and, ultimately, answers.

Initially, it may be necessary for you, the TA, to act out a problem using puppets and any other props or representative equipment. Children may be confident in sorting out a real-life problem in the playground, but once inside the numeracy lesson, it cannot be assumed that they will launch into role play.

As children become more familiar with acting out problems, the lesson could be introduced by using role play, or during the plenary, a group of children could act out one of their answers. This makes the children focus on deciding what the important parts to represent are, how they may be represented or acted out and how they have used this in their answers.

Speaking and listening strategies

Children learn mathematics through listening to others and talking about their learning. By listening to other people's thoughts and ideas we fine tune what we regard as important and adjust our own thinking accordingly.

The use of mathematical vocabulary plays an important part in understanding and describing mathematical concepts – you can provide a definition for a word but children need to figure out when to apply it and what it means by using it and even misusing it on regular basis. When introducing new vocabulary, ask pairs of children to discuss and agree a definition and, over time, build up their own vocabulary book.

Here are some ideas that you could try (some of these have been adapted from *Year 2 Maths Out Loud* by Sara Fielder, BEAM, 2006).

Solver and recorder

Working in pairs, one person is identified as the solver. When given a calculation or problem, the solver must think, then verbalize, their initial hunch, their strategies to find an answer, the process, the calculation required, and so on. At this point, they are the only person speaking and cannot be interrupted by their partner. Their partner acts as the recorder, jotting, writing or drawing what the solver is describing. Choose either the solver or recorder to feedback. The advantage of this is that both children will have to understand the process in order to verbalize it.

Talk partners

Pairs of children work collaboratively on a given problem or calculation. For example, during group work children are asked to identify and name a particular two-dimensional shape. Working with a partner they discuss the problem together. Alternatively, children are asked to talk to a partner for two minutes to discuss initial thinking on a given problem, then respond together. The advantage with this way of working is that less confident children can share with and gather a range of ideas from more confident pupils.

One example of using this technique in practice is to give pairs of children a paper plate. On the paper plate place five two-sided, two-coloured beans. The pairs take turns to throw the beans up in the air and ensure they land on the plate. The pair discusses the different ways that the beans land each time. Ask the pair to investigate the total number of different combinations that can be made.

The children devise their own strategies to record what they have thrown on the plates. You will need to circulate among the pairs, ensuring that everyone has a go at throwing the beans. If discussion between pairs is difficult, prompt with questions such as, 'Have the beans landed showing the same colours each time?' 'If not, what has been different?' 'If you had five red beans, how many white beans would there be?'

After ten minutes, ask each pair to state how many combinations they believe there to be and accept all answers neutrally. Invite feedback and record some of the different combinations. If a combination is repeated, leave it until one of the children notices – if they do not notice, draw their attention to the same number of reds and whites.

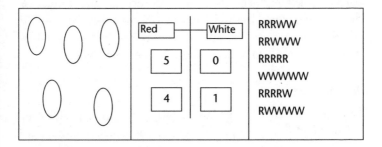

Ask the pairs to discuss which method of recording they prefer and why. Ask them to record the six different combinations as calculations. The pairs can throw the beans and choose whether the red or white bean represents the first number or second number in the calculation.

Solutions – this is always one plus the number of beans, so with five beans there are six combinations. When the beans fall on the plate, this is one combination, plus you can turn each bean over once. You are not taking *order* into account, i.e. in this activity RRRWW and WRRRW are the same combination.

Lolly sticks

Write the children's names on lolly sticks (one name per stick). Instead of children putting their hands up when they have an answer, randomly select a lolly stick. The child whose name has been selected must answer the question, contribute ideas towards a solution or present their strategy of working. Alternatively, if working with a small group, write the children's names on different faces of a dice and roll the dice to decide who will speak.

An object of status

The child that holds the object has the status of being the only person to speak and convey ideas, strategies and answers. When the child holds the object the rest of the group must listen. You or the child can choose the next person to speak. Objects should be interest and age appropriate, for example, a toy or a ball.

Think, pair and share

Initially, children work individually. After a few minutes they then work in pairs, sharing their individual work and extending their knowledge further. To avoid the pairs sharing misconceptions, each pair then discusses with another pair. You could keep doubling the size of the group, until the whole group is openly discussing the problem.

Peer tutoring

Pair a more able child with a less able, less confident child. The more able child acts as the teacher who must explain, model, illustrate and demonstrate a particular mathematics objective. This strategy benefits the 'tutor' who must grasp why the other person does not understand, and think about the aspects that are important to convey meaning. The tutored child benefits from having a friend/child explain and may feel more confident to express their difficulties.

Giving instructions

Erect a barrier from a piece of cardboard or large board. The screen blocks sight of each other's work. One child must instruct the other to carry out drawing, or to make or write something – as there are no visual clues, the child must use correct vocabulary and think about the clarity of the instructions. For example, one child builds a simple model from six interlocking cubes; the other must make the same model following the verbal instructions.

An example of this technique in practice is to organize the children into pairs. One person wears a PE band. The child wearing the band must close their eyes – or could wear a blindfold or face the back of the room. Their partner must memorize a pattern that is drawn on the board.

After one minute the pattern is covered up and the child asks their partner to open their eyes and draw what they describe. Allow five minutes for the drawing before revealing the pattern again so that the pairs can discuss what was accurately drawn and what remained incomplete. Encourage children to use language only. It is very tempting to trace the shape or position with a finger.

Intervene if the describer gets frustrated with the drawer for misinterpreting their instructions or if vague or incomplete instructions annoy the drawer.

Assigning roles

A problem has been set and children have been asked to work in groups of four. It is common for someone in the group to lead and someone to be uncooperative or not contribute. Assigning roles in the group helps to avoid this. For example, one person is allocated the role of the recorder, another is the group leader, another the presenter, and so on. Make badges with the titles of the roles clearly displayed for children to wear.

Try some of the pair and group work suggested here. Make notes on which ones the children enjoyed and responded to best.

Towards an effective written calculation method

Numeracy is a life skill and so having a repertoire of strategies enables you to cope with the practical mathematical demands of everyday life, such as telling the time, making a purchase or reading a timetable. This skill starts as a child and will carry on into adulthood.

At school you would have been taught to add, multiply, subtract and divide. But did you fully understand the mathematics behind the methods, or did you just learn the rules? Today, children are not only encouraged to calculate quickly and efficiently but to know how and why a particular method works and how it can be applied to a problem.

Mathematics is a mental activity – it takes place in the head, even when it is written down. With a variety of mental strategies children will learn to distinguish between the appropriateness of using mental, pen and paper or calculator methods for calculations. Children will be able to reason and explain their method of calculation.

Can you mentally add together 56 and 19?

Did you use one of the following methods?

56 + 20 = 76 76 − 1 = 75	50 + 10 = 60 6 + 9 = 15 60 + 15 = 75	60 + 20 = 80 80 − 4 − 1 = 75	56 + 4 + 5 = 65 65 + 10 = 75

Or did you use a different method?

If you are working out that calculation mentally, there is no right or wrong way of doing it; some methods are quicker and possibly easier, but how you arrive at the answer is personal. Try an activity like this with a group of children and discuss the various methods of working out the answer.

So how would we describe the mental strategies that have been used? Children may be confident to say what they did, but when asked why they may struggle to use mathematical vocabulary.

Methods for calculation

What different strategies are taught in school? (Sometimes the words for the strategies are not taught.)

Partitioning

The place value of the numbers is used so that parts of the numbers can be added separately, for example, the tens then the ones.

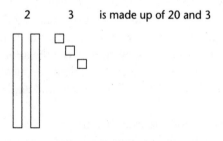

2   3   is made up of 20 and 3

Using pairs of numbers/number bonds

The calculation can be rearranged or jotted over to join up recognizable pairs that are multiples of 10. For example:

6   +   4   = 10

Or, older children can recognize pairs of numbers that can be made to multiples of 10:

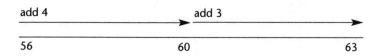

$$2 + 5 + 18 + 19 + 5 + 1 + 3$$

Compensation

This is rounding a number to the nearest ten then adding the rounded numbers. An adjustment must be made at the end so as not to add too much.

For example: 37 + 9 is quicker as 37 + 10 = 47, then 47 − 1 = 46.

Bridging

Again, one-digit numbers may be partitioned and then the parts are added on in steps – up to the next tens number and beyond.

For example: 56 + 7. The 7 is split into a 4 and 3.

add 4	add 3
56	60	63

Using doubles or near doubles

Having rapid recall of doubles can certainly speed up a calculation, but the strategy is likely to be combined with rounding up numbers. Take, for example, the calculation 25 + 26.

$$Double\ 25 = 50$$

$$50 + 1 = 51.$$

Changing the order

When given a calculation such as 7 + 34 children should recognize that it is quicker, easier and they are less likely to make mistakes if they add the smaller number on to the larger one, so it is easier to add 34 + 7.

Counting up or complementary addition

When two numbers are close together and the difference is to be found, it is quicker and more efficient to count up. For example, 2001 – 1998 can be carried out quickly when children recognize these numbers are not far apart in the number system, and they can consequently count up to find the difference.

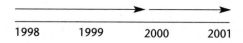

1998	1999	2000	2001

When children are confident at manipulating numbers in order to carry out calculations in their head or with jottings, then they can progress to more formal written methods. The mathematics behind the method must be understood in order for it to be used and applied to larger calculations.

Written methods for addition

It is likely that when we mentally add two-digit numbers together we add the largest part – the tens – first:

$$34 + 27$$
$$\text{So } 30 + 20 \text{ then } 4 + 7.$$

When moving on to written addition set out in columns, this mental image cannot be supported, as the ones must be added first – and so rules start to then be applied.

To show children how each column is added, and emphasize its place value, the first method for column addition looks like this:

```
  68 +
  93
 ───
  11  (8 + 3)
 150  (60 + 90 or 6 tens plus 9 tens)
 ───
 161  (so 68 + 93 is 161)
```

Which then progresses to:

```
  68 +
  93
 ───
 161
   1
```

Are the following mistakes familiar?

```
 127 +
 · 63
 ────
 1810
```

The position for writing the 'carried' ten has been confused and appears as part of the answer.

```
 127 +
  63
 ────
 180
```

The ten has been 'carried' but has been forgotten to be added to the 20 and 60 when adding the tens column.

```
259 +
373
911
 42
```

The ones, rather than the tens, have been 'carried' to the next column.

You may find you are supporting children who do not fully understand place value. They will need visual reinforcement, so you will need to use the Base 10 or Dienes apparatus and set out the sum 68 + 93 as:

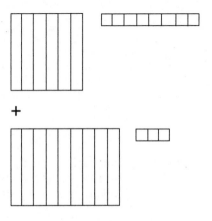

This can then progress to:

```
        60   8 +
        90   3
        10   1
   100  50   0
   100  60   1
```

Alternatively, show children how to add using a number line that encourages use of many of the mental strategies already described. So, 368 + 493 would be shown as:

Here the 8 was partitioned as 7 to bridge to the next 10 and then the remaining 1 was added. The 60 was then added, followed by the 300.

A different way might be:

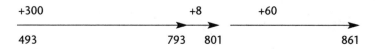

In both examples, children must have a good understanding of number, i.e. place value, the position of numbers in the number system, recall of pairs of numbers, and so on, before attempting to calculate.

Subtraction

Subtraction is a more complex concept to understand. Young children understand subtraction as physically taking something away. If this idea is ingrained then confusion occurs when children move on to written calculations such as 23 – 16 without the use of physical objects.

We could actually take away say, 178 marbles from 326, but it would take a long time and mistakes would be easy to make.

The subtraction can be physically demonstrated using Base 10 or Dienes equipment.

For example, 48 – 25

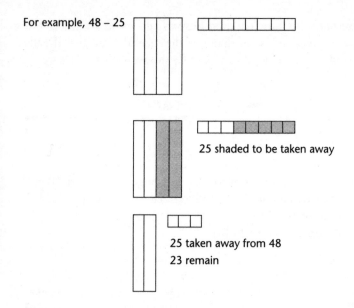

25 shaded to be taken away

25 taken away from 48
23 remain

Children become confused when the calculation is set out with the number to be removed underneath (how can it be taken away when the numbers do not disappear?).

For example:

48 –
25

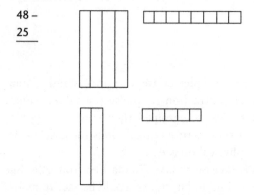

It is just convention that the number to be subtracted/the number at the bottom of the subtraction is written, as it remains intact throughout the calculation.

The use of Dienes or Base 10 as a visual aid helps to explain the mathematics behind this 'formal' written method of subtraction. Children learning this method, known as decomposition, must understand and use the 'rules' to apply to different calculations.

Rule 1

When the digits of the number to be subtracted are smaller than the other number the calculation is straightforward and each part is subtracted in turn, first the ones, then the tens, then the hundreds. For example, 563 – 241 we can visualize as:

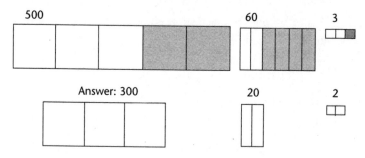

We say: '3 subtract 1 is 2' and write the 2 under the ones' column, '60 subtract 40 is 20' and this is written under the tens' column. Lastly, '200 is subtracted from 500' which is written under the hundreds' column. So the answer is 322.

We can write this as:

$$
\begin{array}{ccc}
500 & 60 & 3\,- \\
200 & 40 & 1 \\
\hline
300 & 20 & 2
\end{array}
$$

This can be shortened to:

$$
\begin{array}{r}
563\ - \\
241 \\
\hline
322
\end{array}
$$

Rule 2

When one or two digits in the bottom number/number to be subtracted are larger than the top digits then the top number needs to be decomposed or broken up into its place value and partitioned in a different way.

For example:

$$563 - 278$$

Stage 1 is to lay out the place value equipment to represent the calculation.

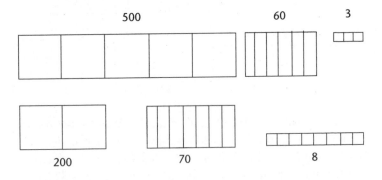

Stage 2 is to break up the place value to support the digits in the top number, i.e. make them larger – note 400 and 150 and 13 is the same as 563.

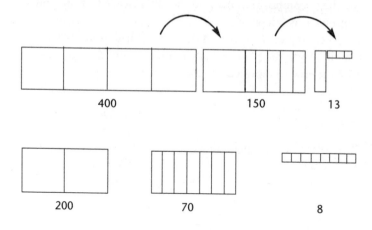

Stage 3 is to carry out the subtraction: 8 from 13, 70 from 150 and 200 from 400.

It is likely to be written, at first, like this:

563 – 278

```
500  60   3 –          ⌐50⌐           ⌐400⌐
200  70   8         500  6̸0  13 –     500 150 13 –
_____         200  70   8       200  70   8
                    _____       _____
                                      200  80   5
```

Before being seen and written like this:

```
    4  15  13 –
    5̸  6̸   3
   _____
    2   8   5
```

Rule 3

Many children may feel secure at subtraction until they try to tackle a question where the number to be subtracted from has a zero as a place holder, such as 507 or 2,001. In order to carry out the decomposition method the child needs to fully understand what is happening.

For example: 203–165. First, the calculation is set out visually using the place value equipment, and discussion may arise on how to represent the lack of tens.

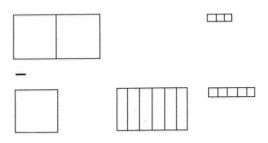

Secondly, the number needs to be decomposed or broken up to ensure that the digit in the top number is larger than that on the bottom so that subtraction can take place.

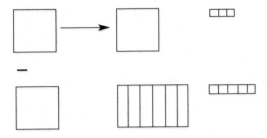

Although the hundreds have been broken up and one hundred has been moved as ten tens into the tens' column, the calculation cannot yet start as three units remain too small. Therefore, the third stage is to break up the ten tens and move one ten to make thirteen units – the 8 can then be subtracted. Nine tens are then left in the middle column and six tens can then be taken away. The hundreds are cancelled out.

Decomposition is commonly taught in primary school. It offers children a quick, reliable method that once learned can be applied to larger numbers and decimals. However, errors are common as 'rules' get muddled or incorrectly applied. The following show common calculation errors – are there any others you are familiar with?

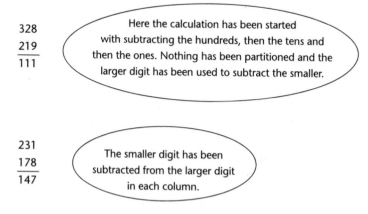

```
328
219
---
111
```

Here the calculation has been started with subtracting the hundreds, then the tens and then the ones. Nothing has been partitioned and the larger digit has been used to subtract the smaller.

```
231
178
---
147
```

The smaller digit has been subtracted from the larger digit in each column.

In Key Stage 1 children are encouraged to mentally count on or up from one number to another when subtracting; for example, 25 – 19 as 19 to 20 and then on to 25. In order to know how many numbers have been counted on, a running total needs to be kept, using fingers or jottings. Mathematically, children are finding the difference between two numbers.

Although less common now than in the past, shopkeepers or market stallholders would return change by counting up from the cost price to the amount given – for example, 19p to 20p and on to 25p, so giving 6p change. They are finding the difference between two amounts of money.

The difference between two numbers can be calculated by counting up or back along a number line. In Key Stage 1 this may be a marked number line, but as children get more confident with the position of the numbers in the number system it can be substituted with an empty line filled in with the numbers that the children choose to use for the calculation.

The advantage of using a number line is that it can be used to subtract, for example, decimals, money and large numbers of any amount. The same 'rule' can be applied to find the difference between any two numbers.

For example: 326 – 178

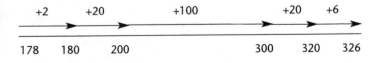

Or for 32.6 – 17.8

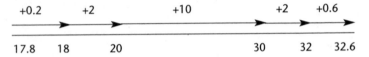

Or for £3.26 – £1.78

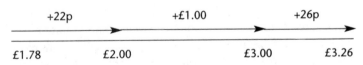

Remember always to use the correct vocabulary when teaching subtraction to children.

Correct vocabulary	Incorrect vocabulary
Partition	Borrow (you never pay it back!)
Decompose	
Change	
Exchange	
Break up	

Multiplication

How would you read this question? 3 × 4 = ?

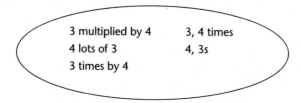

3 multiplied by 4   3, 4 times
4 lots of 3   4, 3s
3 times by 4

Look at the range of language that children will experience and be confused by. The first number is the multiplicand (the number that is added to itself several times), the second is the multiplier.

multiplicand		multiplier		product
3	×	4	=	12

What is the visual image you have for it?

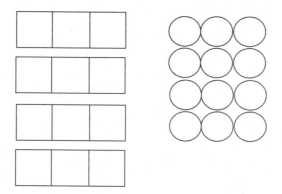

Or

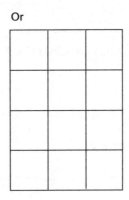

These visual images are forms of 'arrays' or formations that link a visual representation for multiplication to area.

So if we know 3 × 4 = 12, we also know that the area of a piece of paper 3cm by 4cm is 12cm squared. Children need to feel and see multiplication, otherwise, for many, learning 3 × 4 by rote becomes an isolated fact that cannot be used and applied to other learning.

Try this activity to support children in visualizing the times tables facts – children cut out, rearrange, label and keep arrays for the three-times table facts, for example:

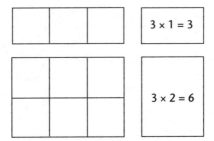

Ask questions such as:

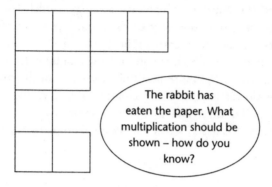

The rabbit has eaten the paper. What multiplication should be shown – how do you know?

But what about 25 × 7? Many children may need to cut out the array for this calculation from squared paper showing an image of 25cm by 7cm. Counting every square is a time-consuming business, so encourage children to divide up the rectangle into sections and find the area of each section. Children may be more confident at multiplying by 10 and 5 than 25.

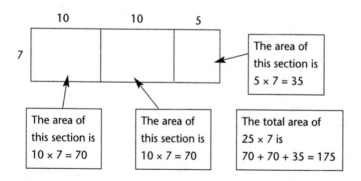

The area of this section is 10 × 7 = 70

The area of this section is 10 × 7 = 70

The area of this section is 5 × 7 = 35

The total area of 25 × 7 is 70 + 70 + 35 = 175

How does this lead to a written method? The grid method requires an understanding of partitioning, place value and addition. The National Numeracy Strategy model described below assumes only one way to partition, but as we can see from above, the numbers can be partitioned in any way, ensuring that the children are multiplying by numbers they are confident with – the more partitions there are in the calculation, the slower it will be but children will have the understanding to link the visual area to the final answer.

The method as described in the National Numeracy Strategy is as follows:

38×17

	30	8
10	300	80
7	210	56

$300 + 210 + 80 + 56 = 646$

For those children needing further support, this could also be partitioned and labelled as:

	10	10	10	8
10	100	100	100	80
7	70	70	70	56

$100 + 100 + 100 + 70 + 70 + 70 + 80 + 56 = 646$

The potential problems with this grid method are in adding up the sections or in the slowness due to lack of recall of times tables' facts. If you are aware of these potential problems you will be able to think of strategies to avoid common mistakes.

An alternative to the grid method of multiplication is a vertical method. For example:

```
    38  ×
     7
   ─────
   210       30 × 7
    56        8 × 7
   ─────
   266
```

The progression here is to move on to two digits by two digits, first expanded to show the parts of the calculation, and then on to 'carrying' digits.

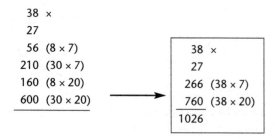

```
  38  ×
  27
  56  (8 × 7)
 210  (30 × 7)
 160  (8 × 20)
 600  (30 × 20)
 ──────────────
```

→

```
  38  ×
  27
 266  (38 × 7)
 760  (38 × 20)
 ─────
1026
```

Division

What language do we use when talking about division?

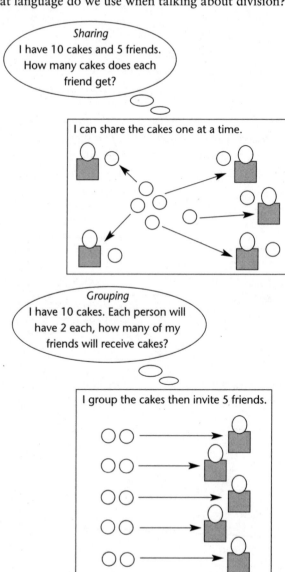

The confusion children have with division is often over these two concepts. From an early age children's experience of division is through physically sharing out objects, but this is not a practical method when dividing larger numbers, such as 643 objects divided between 19 people.

So in division, the progression is related to using multiples of the divisor and repeatedly subtracting these from the dividend, then counting the number of multiples subtracted.

dividend		divisor		quotient
10	/	2	=	5

This can initially be modelled along a number line.
For example:

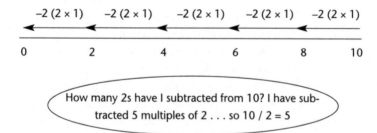

How many 2s have I subtracted from 10? I have subtracted 5 multiples of 2 . . . so 10 / 2 = 5

For larger dividends such as 78 / 3 it would take too much time to subtract 3 each time. Still using a number line, the progression is to take away multiples of 3 that the child knows.

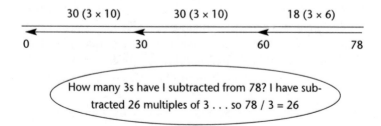

How many 3s have I subtracted from 78? I have subtracted 26 multiples of 3 . . . so 78 / 3 = 26

Although the number line may be used initially, the National Numeracy Strategy encourages children to move on to a vertical representation of division.

So 78 / 3 would be written as:

Divided by 3	78
3 × 10	30
	48 (78 – 30)
3 × 10	30
	18 (48 – 30)
3 × 6	18
	0 (18 – 18)

I have subtracted 10 and 10 and 6 lots of multiples. So I have subtracted 26 lots of 3 from 78 . . . so 78 / 3 = 26

The progression with this method of division is in the number of steps it takes to reduce the dividend to the lowest number – back to zero or to the lowest possible remainder.

Potential problems with this method are in laying out the calculation and performing the subtraction correctly.

For those children who fully understand the concept of division and have a secure understanding of place value and partitioning, the short method can be used to speed up calculation. For example:

$$\begin{array}{r} 168 \\ \hline 4 \overline{)672} \end{array}$$

Stage 1 – 400 (which is the largest whole hundreds number) is divided by 4 to give 100 which is represented by the 1 in the hundreds place. There is a remainder of 272.

Stage 2 – 240 is the largest tens number less than 270 that will divide exactly by 4. So 240 / 4 = 60, which is represented by the 6 above the line in the tens place. There is a remainder of 32.

Stage 3 – The 32 can be divided exactly by 4 and is represented by the 8 in the units place.

The most successful countries for teaching number avoid premature teaching of standard methods so as not to jeopardize mental calculations. So, bridging between recording part written, part mental methods to standard methods begins only when children can add and subtract reliably any pair of two-digit numbers in their heads. We want to encourage children to see a calculation and first of all say, 'Can I do it in my head?' If they cannot, then they must ask themselves if they can jot parts down to help them work it out quickly in their head or use a written method that they are confident with and understand the reasonableness of their answer.

Think about the language you use when you are talking to children about calculations. Are there expressions you use which might be confusing them? How could you make your explanations clearer?

8

Working with more able mathematicians

Think of a child you have supported whom you would describe as more able.

Now list the reasons why you have chosen that child. What characteristics does he or she display in mathematics to distinguish him/her from other children in the class?

Case study of Henry

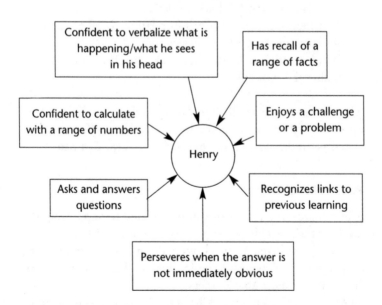

Another way of thinking about the characteristics of the more able mathematicians is to ask yourself:

- Do they have the skills to recall facts easily and apply them to a problem?
- Can they use a reliable algorithm/written method of calculation to apply to addition, subtraction, division and multiplication problems?
- Are they curious to find the answer?
- Can they pose questions to make hypotheses or conjectures – for example, 'I think it is . . . because . . . but I could also see if it . . .' Do they strive to find relationships between numbers and facts?
- Can they prove their answer and explain it to other people?
- Can they link current to previous learning – do they recognize problems that are the same structure/type? Do they ask, 'Is this what I did last week?'
- Can they see new problems in relation to others and use the structure to get to an answer quickly?
- What creative links do they make to other subjects and within the subject?

Able mathematicians will display many of these interlinked characteristics – they are not going to take time and effort to prove an answer if they are not curious to find it in the first place!

Your role as TA

It is common for your work to be directed to supporting the needs of the less able learners. In some schools TAs have been effectively deployed to work with the majority of the class, thus 'freeing up' time for the teacher to challenge and work alongside the most able learners.

Other schools utilize the skills of the TA in acting as a learner alongside the most able group, so posing the questions, setting new challenges, asking for ideas, hypotheses and theories. This group works independently from the teacher.

It may be that the child or children cannot be accommodated within the differentiation of the daily mathematics lesson and need to be offered 'additional' or 'different' work on a one-to-one basis outside the classroom. Some TAs with a subject specialism in mathematics may take groups of children outside the classroom for this 'additional' work with challenges and extensions.

Whichever way your school organizes the role of the TA in supporting more able mathematicians, one thing is clear. It is the child's positive attitude to learning that needs to be maintained.

Leonardo da Vinci was an architect, mathematician, musician, painter, philosopher, geologist, engineer, chef, botanist and physicist. His biographer described him as 'undoubtedly the most curious man who ever lived'. Rumour has it that da Vinci would begin every day by brainstorming 100 questions that during the course of the day he would try to answer – thus clearly displaying a need to 'find out'.

Asking the right questions

So, key vocabulary to stress with the most able pupils are words and phrases such as:

- How do you know?
- What would happen if . . . ?
- Why?
- When would there be a difference . . . ?
- What is the reason for . . . ?
- I know because . . .
- Will it always be . . . ?
- Explain.

As Albert Einstein said, 'The important thing is not to stop questioning.'

At the beginning of a new unit of work ask children to record as many questions as they can that they would like answered over the course of the teaching. By constantly referring back to this list of questions the children can self-assess their own learning and reflect on and change their focus of learning. Alternatively, challenge children to ask the most difficult questions they can think of.

Encourage children to jot their questions, ideas and theories in a working diary or at the back of an exercise book. Entries might include a summary of the activity they are actually doing, any new knowledge they've gained from listening to others, or reflections on what they thought about during the activity. By keeping a written record, they can then refer back to their entries of ideas and feelings if they see a similar problem.

Talking through and answering questions

How does the more able child work? Alone? In a group of similar ability children – but actually, when you observe them, they work alone? Or in pairs?

It may be that you have tried to explain the learning but have failed to do so in a way that a child understands. Often children who have been sitting close to the pupil who hasn't understood are able to explain the learning more effectively. So try encouraging an able mathematician to 'peer tutor' someone who is struggling to understand a particular aspect of the lesson. This way of working benefits the child being taught but also the 'teacher' who must recognize why their peer struggles, unpick and understand the mathematics and then decide on a way to communicate it to another person.

Acceleration, enrichment and extension

You will have often read in the media that a very able mathematician has achieved a pass in a GCSE or A level at a young age. The child will have been taught objectives beyond their chronological age. They are accelerated through the National Curriculum programmes of study to access the necessary learning so, say, a Year 2 child has been taught a Year 4 programme of study.

But what happens next? An 11-year-old child has been accelerated from Key Stage 1 and now has a pass at GCSE. Does the child enter secondary school and move straight to A level or do they 're-sit' some of the objectives taught at Key Stage 3 and the GCSE material? This is a difficult question to answer and it often depends on the child's ability and character. The TA's role here is to ensure that the child retains the enthusiasm and enjoyment of mathematics as well as the ability to communicate and participate alongside their peers.

The most able children need access to an extended 'pitch', i.e. objectives from an older year group. They also need opportunities for extension built into the differentiated activities set in the classroom – for example, the class has been working on a series of calculations and the extension is to build these calculations into a problem or invent a game.

For those children that finish before the others it may be useful to have a list of prompts that extend the thinking. Questions could include:

- What would happen if . . . ?
- Why is this the answer? Why is this not the answer?
- If this is the answer, what might the question have been?
- Is there another strategy you could have used?
- Can you invent your own scenario?

You could encourage the child to carry out their own research on the unit of work, visiting websites or searching the library, or to prepare a presentation for the plenary, summing up the key points of the day's learning. They could also act as a 'teacher', supporting other children in the class.

Having extension questions prepared verbally or in writing will avoid the child becoming bored or disruptive if there is no focus after finishing the work, and will enable the teacher to continue what he or she was doing.

If the child carries out the learning activity quickly and correctly, even if the objectives have been taken from the year above, the task is probably not challenging enough. Challenge through problem-solving and investigation provides enrichment to mathematics that these children may not get if the task is too narrow. Drawing in aspects of other subjects or areas of maths can also enrich the mathematics being studied.

Examples of enrichment activities

Year 1 (2)

This lesson involves measuring and comparing lengths in order to solve a given problem. It starts when the teacher illustrates the concept of concentric objects/shapes such as boxes, Russian dolls, or the rings on an archery target.

Circulate the objects among the group so that they can feel them. Ask children to make three concentric loops from strips of card. The challenge is in measuring and cutting three different lengths, curving them into cylinders and securing them with tape. The cylinders must have enough of a gap to glide in and out of each other and the gap between them should be equal. Afterwards they can be decorated.

You could encourage pairs to work together. They are likely to need a partner to hold the loop while the other secures it. They will need to share a ruler, scissors and tape and develop a system for sharing these resources. This type of lesson could encourage a very able child to work alongside a less able child and discuss the activity and learning together.

After securing three loops, ask the children to investigate how they could use the cylinders to make round boxes. Questions you could ask include:

- What lengths of card did you use?
- What three-dimensional shape have you made?
- Do the loops fit inside each other?
- Why did you design this the way you did?
- Which was the longest, shortest, middle length?
- Did you make more than one attempt?
- Why do you think it went wrong? What did you change?
- Can you explain what you had to make?

Year 4

This lesson involves optimization, i.e. making the most from the money available. It is an activity that could be carried out alone as long as there are opportunities to discuss the task.

The teacher introduces a context, 'You are asked to refurbish your bedroom. The area of the room is 10m squared and you have £500 to spend. What will you buy?'

The children are provided with catalogues or prepared items with prices. An extra challenge can be set by asking the more able child to make a scale model or drawing of the bedroom and then use the measurements provided in the product information section to draw the furniture to scale. The child is tackling a range of mathematics here: area, ratio/scale, addition and subtraction, problems relating to money, and so on.

Questions you might ask include:

- How will you know that bed will fit?
- How much have you spent so far?
- You have bought a bed; do you have enough money for a chair? If not, where will you sit?
- Where is the door? Will it open?
- How is your real bedroom designed? Would you change anything in light of this activity?

Year 5

The more able child is likely to know and recall the times tables with ease. While the rest of the class is practising this rapid recall, challenge the child to make a 'divisibility booklet', explaining the rules and providing examples for each times table. The booklet can be decorated and/or illustrated and displayed in the book corner for the whole class. You could use the mental and oral starter for this activity while the teacher works with the rest of the class.

Whether your school calls these children 'gifted', 'able' or 'mathematically promising', their talents need to be identified, acknowledged and supported. The teacher may plan provision for the child but it may be you, the TA, who offers the challenging questions and prompts towards analytical thinking and reasoning. The challenge for you will be to know when to intervene and ask the questions. There also needs to be a willingness to admit that you are not sure of the answer and require the child to explain, illustrate or role-play their solution. Above all, your role is to channel the energy and enjoyment of pursuing divergent tasks and finding solutions.

Consider some of the more able children in your school. Can you think of other ways to expand and enrich mathematics lessons for them?

9

Resources and references

In 2005, the Department for Education and Skills produced a document that set out the basic skills and knowledge that everyone working with children, young people and families should have. These were a common set or core of skills and they have now been incorporated into the induction training for TAs.

General qualifications and courses

There are various qualification routes for TAs set out under the National Qualifications Framework (NQF). The National Vocational Qualification (NVQ) is run in many adult education establishments and is a work-related, competence-based qualification. There are various awarding bodies such as City and Guilds, Edexcel, the Council for Awards in Children's Care and Education (CACHE) and Oxford, Cambridge and RSA Examinations (OCR).

An inexperienced TA will be working at Level 1. The Level 2 NVQ qualification is aimed at those TAs who have been in post for between one and two years – depending on the hours worked in the school. The course can be completed by a portfolio and assessment in one year, and some adult colleges offer day and evening sessions.

At Level 2, the mandatory units of the course reflect the common core skills for TAs, and candidates then select additional optional units which reflect their role in the school. At Level 2 they will always be working under the direction of a teacher.

For those TAs supporting mathematics for the majority of the time the evidence for the portfolio would have to have a subject bias. For example, in the unit 'Help with classroom resources and records' it could be interpreted as 'with numeracy equipment and records'. Options include:

- Support the use of ICT
- Support numeracy activities
- Contribute to the management of pupil behaviour.

The NVQ at Level 3 is aimed at very experienced TAs who have been working in a school for several years and have a good knowledge and understanding of things like planning, assessment and the range of special educational needs.

Most local authorities have available funding to offer a specific course to those new to the profession but are unlikely to deliver extensive training specifically for those new to supporting children in mathematics. The Training and Development Agency's Induction course offers an opportunity to explore the role of the TA in the mathematics lesson, highlights the importance of questioning and the language of mathematics and discusses a range of calculation methods. The module is usually run in one day. Only one of the five days of the Induction course is mathematics specific.

Mathematics-specific training – when supporting children

There may be opportunities to attend in-service mathematics training at your school on a theme such as problem-solving or supporting children with calculation. Local authority consultants, the school inclusion manager or subject leaders may run the sessions. Different authorities offer different levels and types of mathematics training for TAs, which is often dependent on local needs and priorities – it may be useful to contact your local authority for a list of available professional development courses.

There are various 'self-funded' courses available, such as the two-day 'Being an effective teaching assistant in Key Stage 1 or 2 mathematics' from BEAM education (www.beam.co.uk).

Mathematics-specific training – for yourself

If you want to improve your own mathematical skills, there may be opportunities to find out about basic skills numeracy courses, adult education courses or family numeracy sessions from the local authority. The Basic Skills Agency offers a Quality Mark to those institutions consistently delivering quality training.

For those TAs wanting recognition of their abilities, knowledge and understanding of the application of number, a qualification entitled 'Key skills in application of number' is available. Local colleges or centres provide facilities for candidates to sit the online test. Alongside the test, the candidate provides an internally assessed portfolio of evidence showing application of the numeracy skills. The award is equivalent to a GCSE in mathematics.

However, not all continuing professional development may result in a qualification or training outside the workplace. Training should be about your own professional needs and could include:

- visiting other schools to observe TAs carrying out similar jobs
- observing a colleague carrying out a particular task, for example, supporting a child with visual impairment using a range of mathematical resources
- in-school training offered by a line manager or local authority consultant
- peer coaching or tutoring by a more experienced member of staff
- e-learning – exploring some of the websites listed below to gain greater understanding of a particular aspect of work

    ▪ work-shadowing a colleague on a particular aspect of their work, for example, behaviour management within a mathematics lesson.

Published materials and websites

Information on training/self-study

www.dfes.gov.uk/commoncore – this is the published common core of skills and knowledge for all those working with children.

www.tda.gov.uk/partners/supportstafftraining/inductionmaterial – the PowerPoint presentations, trainer's notes and background reading for delivering the teaching assistant induction programme in both secondary and primary schools.

www.tda.gov.uk/support – extensive links and information on training and development opportunities from the Training and Development Agency.

www.move-on.org.uk – if you need a qualification (a Level 2, which is equivalent to a GCSE) in mathematics, this website provides information on nearest test centres, an online preparation test, a 'mock' test and downloadable resources for teaching.

www.basic-skills.co.uk – The Basic Skills Agency defines basic skills as, 'the ability to use mathematics at a level necessary to function and progress at work and in society in general.' The site provides a wealth of resources to support the teaching of basic mathematical skills. It supports the trainer in delivering basic skills, whether in schools, colleges or elsewhere. There is a useful sharing practice section.

www.talent.ac.uk – a 'one stop shop' for those teaching adults and young people with language, literacy and numeracy needs.

www.maths4life.org – Maths4Life focuses on adults learning mathematics from entry level to level 2. The three-year project, aiming to stimulate a positive approach to teaching and learning in mathematics, ran from 2004 to March 2007 and produced a number of resources, including the *Maths4Life Thinking Through Mathematics* resource pack.

www.learndirect.co.uk – a database of available numeracy courses starting at Level 1 in different UK regions. It provides free advice on careers, training, courses and apprenticeships.

Information on the role of the TA

Aplin, R. (1998), *Assisting Numeracy – A Handbook for Classroom Assistants*. London: BEAM

DfES (2000), *Working with teaching assistants: a good practice guide*. London: DfES (DfES 0148/2000)

DfES (2005), *The effective management of teaching assistants to improve standards in literacy and mathematics*. (DfES 1228-2005G)

National Teacher Resource Panel (2006), *The active engagement of teaching assistants in teaching and learning*. London: DfES

www.teachernet.gov.uk/wholeschool/teachingassistants – extensive information on the role of a higher level teaching assistant and guidance on cover supervision.

Information specific to supporting mathematics teaching and learning

Askew, M., Ebbutt, S. and Mosley, F. (2001), *Teaching Mental Strategies (Years 3 and 4)*. London: BEAM Education

DfES (2006), *Primary Framework for literacy and mathematics*. (DfES 02011-2006BOK-EN)

Fielder, S. (2004), *Step-by-step Addition. (M770), Step-by-step Subtraction. (M771), Step-by-step Multiplication. (M772), Step-by-step Division. (M773)*. London: PCET

Ollerton, M. (2004), *Getting the Buggers to Add Up*. London: Continuum

Ollerton, M. (2007), *100+ Ideas for Teaching Mathematics*. London: Continuum

QCA (1999) *National Curriculum for England* (QCA/99/460)

QCA (2000) *Curriculum Guidance for the Foundation Stage* (QCA/00/587)

Koshy, V. (2001), *Teaching Mathematics to Able Children*. London: David Fulton Publishers

Koshy, V. (1995), *Infant Challenges: Enrichment starting points for able children 4–7 years old*. London: Elephas Publications

Websites

www.standards.dfes.gov.uk – online information not just for numeracy but also aspects of inclusion including supporting gifted and talented learners, children learning English as an additional language and pupils with special educational needs. Click on the 'numeracy' link for up-to-date and previously issued publications as well as information and guidance on planning and the implementation of the revised Numeracy Framework.

www.ncaction.org.uk – online National Curriculum with very useful portfolios of work at Key Stages 1 and 2. There is actual children's work alongside commentary and advice on assessment.

www.qca.org.uk – the Qualifications and Curriculum Authority maintains and develops the National Curriculum, the end of Key Stage tests and accredits and monitors other qualifications such as those in the workplace.

www.beam.co.uk – provides a free downloadable 'problem of the month' for different year groups, as well as online information about courses and resources.

www.bbc.co.uk/jam – the digital brain part of the BBC website provides challenging problems and investigations, from revising and changing arrays, to travel through secret tunnels and programming a rabbit to jump along a number line.

www.atm.org.uk – the site of the Association of Teachers of Mathematics provides lots of information on current mathematics issues, research, ideas and resources.

www.nrich.maths.org – a variety of articles, problem-solving challenges and games for different Key Stages. It also has a thesaurus that can be used as a dictionary and as a tool to translate a mathematical word into Danish, Finnish, Hungarian, Lithuanian, Polish, Slovak and Spanish.

www.counton.org – a wealth of information and links to other mathematics websites. Features include a dictionary, GCSE practice guidance, a 'problem' bank and latest news.

www.worldclassarena.org – international work and tests for the very able and gifted pupils.

www.brunel.ac.uk – research and development centre for Brunel Able Children's Education (BACE) Centre.

www.nagty.ac.uk – the National Academy for Gifted and Talented Youth, for children from 11 years.

Glossary of terms

Algorithm – the sum or calculation, for example 23 + 56 or 2003 × 45.

We refer to the word 'sum' when using addition and 'calculation' for addition, subtraction, division and multiplication.

Array – the visual arrangement for a multiplication calculation. It is often represented as circles or squares – for example, 3 × 2 can be shown as two rows of three circles.

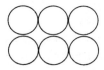

Base 10 – the equipment, made of wood or plastic (often purple or blue) that can be used to represent the place value of numbers. 1,000 is represented by a solid cube, the 100 represented as a flat square, 10 as a stick and 1 as a small cube. If you place 10 small cubes in a line, they would be the same length as the stick; 10 sticks placed alongside each other would be the same size/width as the square; 10 squares placed on top of each other would be the same dimensions as the large cube.

The equipment can be purchased through many school catalogues. It may also be called Dienes, named after the person who devised the resource.

Bridging – a method of calculation whereby the tens numbers (10, 20, 30 . . .) or hundreds numbers (100, 200, 300 . . .) are crossed. For example: 26 – 7.

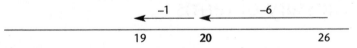

19	**20**	26

In this calculation you have to bridge/cross back past the 20 to take the number away.

Cardinality – the idea that the last number counted represents the number of objects in that set.

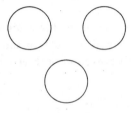

When you count the above set of circles you say 'one' and point to the first, 'two' and point to the second, and 'three' and point to the last. You know you have counted all the circles, so you stop counting. The last number said was three so you know there are three circles in the above set.

Compensation – a method of calculation where you round up a number to the nearest ten, then add the rounded numbers and make an adjustment at the end so that you haven't added too much.

Cuisenaire rods – these are rods of different lengths, often made of wood, that represent different numbers. Cuisenaire was the mathematician who designed this resource. They can be used for ordering, identifying numbers and simple calculations.

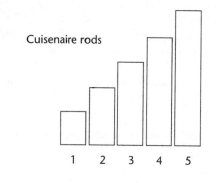

Cuisenaire rods

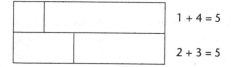

1 + 4 = 5

2 + 3 = 5

Decomposition – a method for breaking down a number to aid a calculation. For example, in a subtraction calculation, the 'top' number is broken up and redistributed so that the 'bottom' number can be subtracted.

```
                    4  11  14  ——→ This is now 400, 110 and 14
    5   2   4  ——→  5̶   2̶   4  ——→ This was 500, 20 and 4
    2   3   7        2   3   7
```

When the 'top' number has been decomposed you can see that 400 and 110 (shown as 11 tens) and 14 is the same as 500 and 20 and 4.

Dividend – the number to be divided by another number.

Divisor – the number that is being used to share/divide an amount or number.

12	/	3	=	4
Dividend		divisor		quotient

Multiplicand – the number that is multiplied by another number.

Multiplier – the number used to increase/multiply an amount.

3	×	4	=	12
multiplicand		multiplier		product

Numicon™ – the trade name for a resource used for number recognition and for understanding the relationships between numbers, for example, that the numbers go up in ones. The resource tends to be used in Foundation Stage, early Key Stage 1 and in special schools. It is similar to Cuisenaire in the respect that it consists of coloured plastic pieces that can be positioned to show equivalents. For more information see www.numicon.com/

One-to-one correspondence – when counting you need to ensure each object has been included. To do this we point at an object and say the corresponding number almost simultaneously. For example:

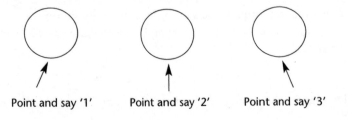

Point and say '1'   Point and say '2'   Point and say '3'

Partition – breaking numbers up into parts to aid calculation. For example, in the calculation 34 × 56 we can part the tens from the units in both numbers and multiply the parts in turn.

×	30	4
50		
6		

or in the following calculation 17 + 7, the 7 has been broken into 3 and 4.

17	20	24
	+3	+4

Place value – the value of the position of the digit, so in the number 234, 200 is represented by the 2, 30 is displayed as 3 and 4 is shown as 4.

Product – the answer to a multiplication calculation. For example, the product of 3 × 4 is 12.

Quotient – the answer to a division calculation. For example, the quotient of 12 / 3 is 4.

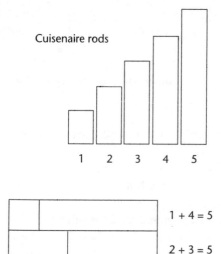

Cuisenaire rods

1   2   3   4   5

1 + 4 = 5

2 + 3 = 5

Decomposition – a method for breaking down a number to aid a calculation. For example, in a subtraction calculation, the 'top' number is broken up and redistributed so that the 'bottom' number can be subtracted.

```
              4  11  14  ──►This is now 400, 110 and 14
    5  2  4  ──► 5̶  2̶  4 ──►This was 500, 20 and 4
    2  3  7       2  3  7
```

When the 'top' number has been decomposed you can see that 400 and 110 (shown as 11 tens) and 14 is the same as 500 and 20 and 4.

Dividend – the number to be divided by another number.

Divisor – the number that is being used to share/divide an amount or number.

12	/	3	=	4
Dividend		divisor		quotient

Multiplicand – the number that is multiplied by another number.

Multiplier – the number used to increase/multiply an amount.

3	×	4	=	12
multiplicand		multiplier		product

Numicon™ – the trade name for a resource used for number recognition and for understanding the relationships between numbers, for example, that the numbers go up in ones. The resource tends to be used in Foundation Stage, early Key Stage 1 and in special schools. It is similar to Cuisenaire in the respect that it consists of coloured plastic pieces that can be positioned to show equivalents. For more information see www.numicon.com/

One-to-one correspondence – when counting you need to ensure each object has been included. To do this we point at an object and say the corresponding number almost simultaneously. For example:

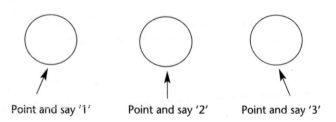

Point and say '1'   Point and say '2'   Point and say '3'

Partition – breaking numbers up into parts to aid calculation. For example, in the calculation 34 × 56 we can part the tens from the units in both numbers and multiply the parts in turn.

×	30	4
50		
6		

or in the following calculation 17 + 7, the 7 has been broken into 3 and 4.

+3 →	+4 →
17	20	24

Place value – the value of the position of the digit, so in the number 234, 200 is represented by the 2, 30 is displayed as 3 and 4 is shown as 4.

Product – the answer to a multiplication calculation. For example, the product of 3 × 4 is 12.

Quotient – the answer to a division calculation. For example, the quotient of 12 / 3 is 4.